Everyday Wisdom
for Inspired Teaching

Tim Lautzenheiser

Also by Tim Lautzenheiser

The Joy of Inspired Teaching

The Art of Successful Teaching

Music Advocacy and Student Leadership:
Key Components of Every Successful Music Program

Everyday Wisdom for Inspired Teaching

Tim Lautzenheiser

GIA Publications, Inc.
Chicago • www.giamusic.com

Book layout and design: Martha Chlipala

G-6652
Copyright © 2005, GIA Publications, Inc.
7404 S. Mason Ave., Chicago, IL 60638
www.giamusic.com
ISBN: 1-57999-527-6

Printed in the United States of America.

Dedication

This book is dedicated to YOU and all the caring, sharing souls who have dedicated their lives to working with the most precious natural resource we have: OUR YOUTH. Our planet is better because of your selfless contribution to the TEACHING profession. May you continue to turn knowledge into wisdom by tapping the creative minds of those students who are the benefactors of your lifelong commitment to the world of learning.

Contents

Part One:
The Art of Teaching

Part Two:
Developing an Attitude for Success

Part Three:
Teacher Leadership Skills

Part Four:
Selection and Encouragement of Student Leaders

Author's Thoughts

Most books are designed to be read from beginning to end; however, that is not the case with this text. Simply flip through the index and find the chapter title applicable to your specific interest at the given moment. There is no intended sequence from one chapter to the next, but rather each subject area is a mini book within itself.

I hope the pages ahead will serve as inspiration as you embrace one of history's most noble professions: TEACHING.

Foreword
Michael Kumer

Congratulations and thanks, Tim…you've done it again.

Everyday Wisdom for Inspired Teaching is the rarest of precious gifts: a collection of timeless essays that fully engages the reader in the art of effective teaching. It provokes, uplifts, and inspires interest in anyone truly committed to excellence in teaching and learning.

Tim has written anything but a coffee-table book; it's meant to be well read and thoroughly (and repeatedly) digested until the many profound and invaluable lessons are completely assimilated. (It is one thing for us to learn; it's quite another to apply what we learn. Or, as Tim is fond of saying, "It's not what you can do; it's not what you will do; it's what you *do* do!")

One can read, enjoy, and benefit from these essays as independent, stand-alone entities, or interdependently in a broader context as a philosophy of education. Readers are encouraged to enjoy a single chapter daily (a veritable "one-a-day vitamin" for the mind), begin in the middle, or savor the complete volume sequentially or in reverse order. One also can quickly and easily recall individual chapters, aided immeasurably by Tim's incomparable use of a wide range of literary devices, including acronyms and alliteration. (Two of my personal favorites are "H.E.A.R.T." and "Straight A's"). His remarkable linguistic repertoire constitutes a virtual "how-to" manual for unusually effective pedagogy.

Everyday Wisdom for Inspired Teaching removes barriers that have hindered our understanding of myriad (and complex) learning processes. In Tim's skilled hands, content/context; cause/effect; teaching/learning; subject/object; product/process; cognitive/affective…all melt away as artificial dualities. Instead, they are seen as integral to the whole. As a result, our capacity to enliven the classroom and catalyze the minds of our students is enhanced and enlarged.

And this brings us with blinding clarity to the book's fundamental essence: it is a riotously joyous celebration of Tim's astonishing life of service to others, a life dedicated to opening the hearts, minds, and souls of so many by willingly, enthusiastically, and unconditionally opening his heart, mind, and soul and widely sharing his divinely inspired gifts. Tim, from all of us who continue to learn from you and who are deeply touched by your congruence of thought, word, and deed—congratulations. And thanks, once again.

– April 2005

About Michael Kumer

Michael Kumer is presently serving as the executive director of the Nonprofit Leadership Institute at Duquesne University in Pittsburgh, Pennsylvania. His life reflects a blueprint of success as a master teacher, a successful university administrator, a remarkably gifted speaker, and, above all, an individual who is an exemplary role model for all who are dedicated to making this world a better place. His commitment to excellence is evident in every aspect of his life; above all, he is dedicated to helping others explore their unlimited potential.

We all know the value of a trusted friend—someone who will always listen with an open mind and a sensitive heart, who always offers a sanctuary of support regardless of the situation, and who loves you for "who you are…just as you are." Michael Kumer is, I can proudly say, MY BEST FRIEND.

Thank you, Michael, for assuming the role as my confidant. You continue to be the person who "walks the talk," and you do it with a sense of purpose that benefits all of us who are fortunate enough to be in your presence. I want to be "just like you" when I grow up.

– Tim Lautzenheiser

Acknowledgements

Heartfelt appreciation is extended to:

- All the teachers who were part of my endless educational excursion. Your influence continues to be the guiding force for every choice I make.

- My students, who serve as constant reminders of the awesome responsibility we all face when we assume the role of TEACHER. You are reflections of my daily efforts.

- My mother and father, who, to this day, are there to support and encourage me. Their unconditional love is a gift beyond measure.

- Alec Harris and the GIA Publications family of friends. Not only did you make "the dream come true,"—you wrapped it with a sense of professionalism that has become a trademark of quality recognized by all.

- Andrea, my partner, my soul mate, and the person who continues to make life worth living with a sense of "signature class" unknown in common hours.

Introduction
Alec Harris

I first encountered Tim Lautzenheiser in 1991 at the Iowa Music Educators' convention in Des Moines. I had heard of Tim, of course, but I was flabbergasted after the session.

More than 200 people sat riveted to Tim's every word. By the time the session was over, many in the audience were moved to tears (myself included, and I tend not to be prone to that sort of thing). A huge percentage of those in attendance rushed to speak with Tim after the session.

Tim has the ability to reach out and grab us at a very deep level. He has the gift to remind us why we are committed to the education profession. He knows the obstacles teachers face, and he understands how the day-to-day grind can pull us down. After just one hour with Tim, it felt as if he reached down into that pit of self-doubt and lifted each and every one of us back out again.

I knew then that Tim's message needed to be heard by the widest possible audience, which is why, following that Des Moines clinic, I asked Tim to write his first book. *The Art of Successful Teaching* remains one of the best sellers in GIA's catalog.

Tim continues to travel the United States and the world touching more lives than you'd think would be possible for a human being. In one recent year, Tim led an eye-popping 328 workshops.

And while Tim originally worked only in the field of music education, his message is being heard—and needs to be heard—by an ever-broader audience. This book is intended to reach teachers and administrators beyond the music education field. Anyone who teaches and works with young people stands to benefit tremendously.

If you are reading this book, it is because you have chosen a very special career. Your work allows you to have an enormous positive impact on the lives of young people.

Every chapter in this book will help keep your sights on that critical role without ignoring the day-to-day details.

Whether you digest this book in bite-sized pieces or in one giant gulp, I encourage you to keep returning to it. The wisdom in these pages will resonate differently as you move through your career. Speaking as someone who has benefited from wonderful teachers and programs, thank you so much for taking on this important life mission.

And thank you, Tim, for all you do. Thank you for your vision, your humbleness, and your kindness. The world is a better place because of you.

About Alec Harris

Simply put, this book would not exist had I not met Alec Harris many years ago. While the notion of writing a book had always been somewhat of a distant dream, it wasn't until Alec Harris tracked me down following a clinic presentation at a convention and asked, "Have you ever thought about putting your seminar materials in a book so the ideas could be shared with your fellow teachers in the educational community?" that I seriously considered it. Little did either of us know his incidental inquiry would become the seed of an extraordinary friendship that now spans more than two decades, along with several books added to GIA Publications' catalog.

Alec is not only a trusted guide, but also a staunch supporter of not only the message, but the messenger. His faithful encouragement and positive influence are steadfast certainties along the often-unpredictable writing journey. As a publisher, he is second to none, always ready and willing to extend whatever support is necessary to facilitate the project at hand. As a friend, he contributes a nurturing sense of loyalty that is the foundation of every great partnership.

I'm indebted to Alec Harris, his father Ed Harris, and all the staff at GIA Publications, Inc. I'm particularly honored to have the INTRODUCTION of this book authored by an individual who has contributed so much to my professional career and my personal growth. Thank you, Alec, you are one in many millions.

– Tim Lautzenheiser

Part One:
The Art of Teaching

Chapter 1

The Art of Teaching

The best time to plant a tree is twenty years ago.
The second best time is now!
—African proverb

We're lucky if we have two or three great teachers in our lives! That's the truth! Remember your great ones? If you will take a moment and reflect on those educators who made a lasting impression, you will probably discover it was not the subject material that brought you to the front of your seat, it was the teacher...that magical person who could take technically boring information and make it live, create interest, tickle your inquisitive mind, and bring forth a desire to want more data.

One of the more popular phrases often heard in the halls of schools around the nation is, "If you don't make it as a _____, then you can teach." That has always bothered me...still does! Teaching is an art in its own right. A great teacher can amass information of any kind and have students excited and interested in a topic, not so much because of the topic, but because of the presentation of the material or, if you will, the performance of the teacher.

Being an "expert" on any subject matter does not a teacher make. We all knew college professors who were "international experts" on the given subject matter and wrote the definitive text concerning that very topic. Yet in the classroom, they failed time and time again to teach; they simply lectured. There was no sense of performance or art in conveying this information; in fact, it often seemed a burden to their schedules—they would much rather have been researching or writing. On the other hand, we have all experienced that enthusiastic graduate student who could take the most elementary information and have everyone buzzing about what a fantastic class they were having.

Perhaps the art of teaching can't be taught. We can observe the "great ones" and record their body language, pacing, outlines, etc., but we cannot capture the spontaneity and the sensitivity so crucial to their success. They are artists in the strictest sense of the word, and they are not often recognized for this talent, but overshadowed by others who are in a more visible area.

The true teacher is one who teaches out of a passion for sharing. Teaching is a profession of service to other people. The word "care" seems to suggest the appropriate main theme of the artistic teachers: THEY CARE!

This section of the text is written with this theme in mind —the importance of the need to care.

Chapter 2

What Makes Great Teachers?

The important thing is this: to be able, at any moment, to
sacrifice what we are for what we could become.
—Charles DuBois

If we were fortunate, we all had some teachers who were able to touch something down deep inside us that really determined our thinking about everything. Perhaps they cofirmed a certain belief pattern, influenced the way we handled problems, or caused us to understand a behavioral habit, etc. These were special educators—super teachers gifted in shaping and directing our lives.

No doubt many of us chose to become teachers because of these influential individuals. We wanted to follow in their footsteps and have used them as models in developing our own styles of teaching.

What made these educators different from the other teachers? They went to the same colleges, took the same courses, and parked in the same lot with the other faculty. They suffered the same budget cuts, took their turns at lunch-line duty, and had personal crises. Yet, there was something distinctively different, a certain charisma that separated these teachers from the masses.

Wouldn't it be wonderful if we could identify these qualities and pass them on to all teachers who could, in turn, have an equal impact on their students? Or think about taking a college methods course on "Techniques of Meaningful Life Direction via Classroom Material" or "Creating Personal Fulfillment and Purpose through My Classroom Experience." We would all sign up for those courses! What do you suppose the curriculum would be? What texts would they use? Who would teach the class? Would we study the Bible? Socrates? Plato? Would we do research or do role-playing experiments? How would we gain this important information to ensure effective teaching?

In our educational world we have two basic areas of emphasis: cognitive (skills, facts, measurable information) and affective (attitudes, feelings, conceptual thinking). To help us determine the characteristics of these great teachers, let us be specific in identifying what made them stand out in our assessment of the countless educators who were a part of our formal learning. Take just a moment and remember one or two of your finest teachers, and then focus on the attributes that gave them this personally bestowed honor in your life. The list of qualities will probably look something like this:

1. They were caring.
2. They showed tremendous dedication.
3. They always had time for me.
4. They had a good sense of humor.
5. They could communicate well.
6. They enjoyed their work.
7. They showed personal discipline.
8. They were fair.
9. They demonstrated persistence.
10. They respected me as a person.
(And the list goes on and on...)

If we take this list and divide these qualities into skills and attitudes, it will give us some basis for determining the inherent characteristics of this extraordinary teacher. (Of course, all of this can be argued; however, let's bypass these "either/or" details in favor of coming to some conclusion that can benefit all of us.)

Caring. There's no question about this one. It's an attitude. It takes a certain amount of skill to maintain this attitude, but caring is a choice of behavior.

Dedication. Although maintaining any sort of dedication is a real skill, the people who are dedicated don't learn this from a text. If they weren't dedicated, they wouldn't be reading the texts in the first place. Dedication is an attitude about how we are going to spend our given time and with what intensity level we are going to focus our energy.

Having time to share. Certainly we are talking about a major attitude here. We all have the same number of hours in the day. Any educator can decide how to spend those given hours. We all admire those unique teachers who welcome our personal thoughts and show sincere interest in us beyond the classroom.

Sense of humor. Humor is the shortest distance between two people. The most effective humor stems from the enjoyment of the day-to-day situations that occur right under our noses. In most cases, we can either get upset about what happened or find some humor in it and move on. Humor releases tension; anger causes it. Definitely, a sense of humor is an attitude.

Communication. We read a lot about "communicative skills," and certainly there is a lot to be said for understanding how to communicate. Yet, with all the skills in the world, little is exchanged unless we are ready to accept the responsibility of expressing ourselves. We all make a conscious choice to share or not to share. Therefore, communication becomes a skill fueled by an attitude.

Enjoyment. We may "learn" the habit of enjoyment, but for most people enjoyment is a direct reflection of their attitude. People choose to enjoy opera, football, stamp collecting, gardening, or whatever. They have a positive attitude about what they are doing. Others may learn (skill) all the ins and outs of a particular activity and still never enjoy one moment of their involvement.

Personal Discipline. We all admire and respect the person who is willing to go the extra mile. And we all have this opportunity each and every day. There is no book on how to be disciplined. It is a matter of enforcing our willpower. It's making up our minds to seek excellence. It's an attitude about how we want to live our lives.

Fair. Many times we think of a fair teacher as one who broke existing rules because the rules were unfair in a given circumstance. Perhaps this teacher extended a deadline on a paper, gave extra credit for dedicated service, or even violated a school policy to see you have a better opportunity. Most certainly, this is an attitude about the student's best interests.

Persistence. This wonderful key to success is the very attitude separating those who "know" from those who "succeed." These great examples simply will not give up! When all others throw in the towel (and justifiably so), here comes master teacher with two or three more efforts, which ultimately set the standards for all others. This quality represents a very simple choice: I won't quit! What a tremendous attitude.

Respect. Teachers who respect their students also respect themselves. We cannot give to others what we don't have for ourselves. No academic degree or position can give you respect. Respect is something that comes from within. It is an attitude about oneself that transfers directly to those around us. So often we think attending this or that workshop, clinic, or seminar will make us more effective teachers when, in fact, we should be thinking: this new information will give me more to share with my students via my effective teaching.

As we have discovered, those high-quality mentors were the ones who displayed incredible attitudes. We all have experienced teachers who were knowledgeable (beyond compare) yet totally ineffective in the classroom. We respected their bank of facts but eagerly looked forwa rd to the completion of the class so we could get on with life. Then there were those magical teachers who brought us to the edge of our seats, often in subject areas where we had no specific interest other than getting caught up in the enthusiasm reflected from this compelling force, the teacher!

All of us want to improve our teaching effectiveness. (If we don't, perhaps we're not real teachers in the first place!) There is no question we will continue to sharpen our skills because this is the way we grow, learn, create, and become more qualified to do our best work. These skills offer us the ability to move forward in our purpose. However, these skills are virtually worthless in our educational system unless they are used in the correct fashion and with the proper attitude.

If we are destined to make a positive difference in the lives of our students, then we must develop those qualities that are trademarks of the master teacher: positive, productive attitudes!

The exciting part of all of this lies in the fact that when we accept this reality, we not only become better teachers, we improve our own lives, which in turn allows us to be more effective in the classroom, and the cycle goes on and on. But the truth is: we are the only teacher we have ever had! Let's give ourselves a greater education via great attitudes!

Here's to teaching excellence!

Chapter 3

You Gotta Have H.E.A.R.T.

We make a living by what we get,
but we make a life by what we give.
—Winston Churchill

The seed of this topic came from a student who was asked to write a paper about her most influential teacher. She had to describe what separated this particular educator from all those who had been a part of her school experiences. The last line of the paper succinctly and beautifully put everything into perspective with this sentence: "Above all, Mrs. Taylor had a good heart; that's what made her so special."

Let us examine the qualities and character attributes of a master teacher who has H.E.A.R.T.:

H – HONESTY

Think about the exemplary teachers you admired and respected, those you held in highest esteem. You could always trust them to be honest in their assessment of every situation. They respected truth for the sake of truth, and while their decisions were not always popular, they were the right choices to reinforce the basic values of ethics, integrity, and dignity. They demanded excellence at every level, and they realized building high-quality programs with high-quality people requires a foundation of honesty.

E – ENTHUSIASM

Enthusiasm is not to be confused with the shallow excitement we often associate with lack of substance; quite the contrary, the great teachers exude a passion for their work, their programs, their schools, their communities, and—most of all—their students. Enthusiasm, taken from the Greek language, "en theos" (in the presence of a Divine spirit), is a reflection of the teacher's desire to exchange valuable knowledge that will make a lasting impression on his or her students. Enthusiasm is the spark that ignites the learning process and stimulates intrinsic motivation, opening the mind to an unlimited number of creative processes.

A – ATTITUDE

Did you ever know a great teacher who did not have a positive attitude? Like it or not, students tend to reflect the attitudes of their teachers. Most certainly, the extraordinary teachers raise the bar-of-expectation while modeling a positive attitude of acceptance and a willingness to help others who need extra attention in the learning process. The truly great educators do not have the time or the inclination to play in the game of sarcasm and cynicism; they refrain from being involved in negative conversations, and they devote their time and energies to problem resolution instead of problem recognition. They understand the power associated with a positive role model; thus, their attitude is primary in everything they do and everything they are.

R – RESPONSIBILITY

Master teachers understand the crucial importance of responsibility—"the ability to respond." They do what needs to be done, when it needs to be done, whether they want to do it or not, without anybody asking.

The art of teaching requires a constant focus on self-discipline. Unlike many professionals, the teacher's workday never ends. Although the final school bell completes the official school day, the dedicated educator is always thinking, planning, organizing, and creating more effective and efficient ways to support program growth to benefit the students involved. They are always encouraging others to new heights of achievement, focusing the human potential to provide a healthy atmosphere for safe and meaningful learning experiences, and they are constantly recognizing and rewarding those who are making strides toward the given goals. Simply put, they are there for everyone; they are responsible.

T – TRUSTWORTHINESS

Great educators are "worthy-of-trust." They refuse to take advantage of another individual for personal gains. They do not take shortcuts or unfairly make decisions that would put another person in an uncompromising position. While they stick firmly with their convictions, they are not restricted by outdated policies or myopic rules and regulations. Master teachers are true to their word; they do what they say they will do regardless of the price they must pay. They "walk their talk." The framework of every successful program is based on the trust of the participants who are mirroring the trustworthiness of the teacher.

There you have it, the H.E.A.R.T. of great teachers: Honesty, Enthusiasm, Attitude, Responsibility, and Trustworthiness.

We all have the wherewithal to enjoy and live the H.E.A.R.T. of a great teacher. It requires a personal commitment to practicing these cornerstone characteristics as we go through our daily agendas. Would you like to be remembered as one of the "special teachers" in the lives of your students? If so, "you gotta have H.E.A.R.T."

Chapter 4

The Demand for Excellence

The rung of a ladder was never meant to rest upon, but only to hold a man's foot long enough to enable him to put the other somewhat higher. —**Thomas Henry Huxley**

Everyone wants "the answer"—the answer to everything from installing a garage door opener to dealing with an irate parent. If I just had "the answer," all of my problems would be gone. Peace, freedom from worry, and ecstasy would prevail every moment of every day!

Where does one find "the answer"?

As we look around, it is obvious we all seek this fantastic information, and we all seem to go about it via various avenues: more education, yoga, conference calling, self-abuse, marriage, divorce, remarriage, vegetarian diets, mystic brew, emotional bruises, physical health programs, tanning beds, and R–O–L–A–I–D–S. How do you spell relief?

What does it take to bring us to this wonderful, safe land of success and self-satisfaction?

For everyone who is looking for the "foolproof, absolutely guaranteed, will-never-fail secret," this is not the chapter for you—head back to the tanning beds! This message is for the person who is dedicated to this great profession called teaching. This is for the educator who stumbles and falls, makes mistakes—like locking the keys in the car, and not being able to find the needed insurance paper for the hospital when someone breaks an ankle during the faculty volleyball game. Maybe this is you!

Our job as teachers has been scribed, prescribed, and described to the point that we may not know what we're supposed to do. In spite of all this illusion, we know we are counting on ourselves to be successful in our chosen field of endeavor, and the reflection of our efforts can be seen in our students day in and day out. These observations and evaluations serve as the fuel for our forward progress as well as the "emotional breaks" of self-doubt. We all know that students can make or break our days, and the reality is that they reflect our own attitudes. Therefore, it is of ultimate importance that we institute a high feeling of self-worth in our students and colleagues so we can enjoy this reflection of attitudes.

The one absolute, obvious quality of every great teacher is the ability to communicate the importance of self-discipline to his or her students. They can focus the energy, and as a result, accomplishment jumps to a new level. This creates a greater desire to succeed, and the self-discipline goes up accordingly. It sounds simple, but the really fine teachers know the process is far more complicated. Focusing the energy is an art! What "turns on" one student may "turn off" the next. The very key to opening the lock to a student's unlimited potential may be magically effective on Monday and totally useless on Tuesday. The number of variables controlling this phenomenon is infinite, not to mention the changes you, as an educator, go through each day, which also affect your perspective. So what's "the answer"?

It seems the successful people in the teaching world share one commonalty: the demand for excellence—and they insist on and demonstrate their own persistence in this quest. In common terms, they don't quit 'til they get it right! They all have their own ways of handling their organizational procedures, they use all different kinds of support materials, they may violate every rule in the book, and they may project every attitude associated with "bad teaching," but they succeed time after time. Students will go the extra mile for them 90 percent of the time—and whatever it takes, they somehow seem to meet the call.

Self-discipline produces a feeling of self-worth that generates a higher level of self-discipline, etc., etc., etc. This all leads to a feeling of self-esteem, and because our feelings control our behavior, it stands to reason that someone with high self-esteem is going to behave and perform with a success-oriented focus. The result is success.

Again, it sounds so simple; just work hard...feel good about yourself...and work harder so you can feel even better! Every self-help book will give you that recipe, and you'll put down the book and be ready to move mountains. However...

Here's the part they forgot to mention: Let's work hard...and then fail at our task—do we still feel good? No! In this case, hard work produced a negative feeling. The logical mind quickly asks: do I feel better, or do I feel worse? This is exactly where the break comes between those who make it and those who don't. Most people can rationalize "not doing" almost anything. If we do nothing, we never have to suffer the penalties (the feelings) of failure. We can also stand back and point to where others have failed and brag about being "exempt" because we knew better than to try it in the first place. Sad but true!

It is at this juncture we make the choice for failure or success. The "failure" of the task can be corrected, but if we quit, we're done! The mind will struggle internally. ("If you go again and fail, then you're twice as bad!") The answer: learn from the failure and go right back into the task again. Tackle it from a different angle, get the help of some other people, research another way to go about it, break it down into smaller parts, but don't quit! The importance of the task may be inconsequential, but the feeling you establish is going to be the groundwork for the next problem you face. Simply don't allow feelings of failure to be a part of your thinking pattern. The joy of breakthrough accomplishment is so tremendous that it almost justifies whatever price one must pay.

The bonus of never quitting (as teachers) comes from the role models we set for the many students who are watching us with more learning awareness than most of us want to admit. They see that you, too, run up against obstacles that seem overwhelming; even teachers don't have all the answers, but most search and risk. The feelings of inferiority that dominate the young people's thinking are then evident in our behavior; however, we model for the youth what to do with these feelings: go on in spite of them!

The habits and patterns ingrained during the school years will determine the patterns of life. Although we always instruct—"Grow up...Be mature...Quit acting like a child...Come on, grow up!"—do we ever grow up? Sometimes we imply that when one is "grown up" all the problems of life will have answers at hand, and we will simply live in bliss and happiness. We all know growing up is going to be a process until death. With that in mind, what an opportunity we have in front of us every day to teach, taking the problems of life and turning them into living examples of learning experiences. Each day becomes a lab class of how to handle this wonderful thing called life!

One of the greatest benefits that comes from the demand for excellence is the understood rule that you can't quit until you have achieved. There is no room for anything less. Do we dare ask anything less of our students? Of ourselves?

It is said that we have six to eight failures for every one success. Knowing that, how could we possibly stop after four, five, or even six bad attempts? The payoff could easily be in the next try. When we fall down, it is so easy to lie there and defend why we cannot get back up, but that only supports the failure. Any truly successful person will tell you the temptation to "stay down" never leaves—the mind seems to always throw the temptation right in our faces. Stay down. Don't take any more stupid chances. Everyone else is down, too. You aren't good enough—you'll fall again. People are laughing at you. Who do you think you are anyway?

When this happens, immediately begin to talk to yourself. What made me fall? Where did it hurt? What could I have done differently? Is there anything I can use in this experience to help if I fall again? What's the best way to get up? This very technique of "self-talk" may be the one key factor in establishing a high level of self-discipline. It's a matter of serving as your own cheerleader—focus your own energy and demand excellence from yourself.

As teachers, we must do this for ourselves, but we can also serve as the "surrogate cheerleader" for the students. When we see the fall (fail), we must jump right up and urge them to give it another shot. It is the chance for us to encourage, to give new information, to express feelings, to strengthen our resistance, to teach. Failure is not bad.

We must welcome these instances and focus the energy of the circumstance so we can prepare for the next level. Through all of this effort, we learn, we grow, we expand—and then we can pass that knowledge right back to the students.

In conclusion, the demand for excellence is seen around us every day. Each person interprets this quality, this attribute, in many ways: some with strict rules, some through expressive sharing, some through group dynamics, and many through a combination of all these methods, plus many more. Whatever it takes, the obvious striving for excellence is always predominant. Wonderful teachers just don't quit...and their students mirror this quality. Maybe the students never reach the top of the mountain, but they sure have a magnificent learning experience on the way up!

The answer? Don't quit! The way not to quit? Don't quit! And when you can justify quitting in every logical way: don't quit! And when you're tired and you feel like nobody really cares: don't quit! And when all else fails, take R–O–L–A–I–D–S, then get back to work—you're setting the pace for all of us!

Chapter 5

Dealing with "It's Good Enough..."[1]

When we think positively and imagine what we want,
we risk disappointment; when we don't, we ensure it.
—Lana Limpert

- Doesn't the title make you cringe?

- Isn't the phrase, "It's good enough," offensive to your sense of educational integrity?

- Aren't you tempted to impulsively react in a defensive manner when a student resorts to this worn-out old excuse?

Why would anyone ever claim "it's good enough"? We know the pathway to excellence is never-ending, and yet we are constantly searching for teaching techniques that will stimulate our students to reach a higher level of personal achievement, to push them beyond the perceived "it's good enough."

Without question, every individual has an unlimited supply of undeveloped (or underdeveloped) talent. Even the masters are constantly pushing themselves to a higher level of skill attainment. If we know we can be more proficient, what keeps us from developing to the next level of awareness or understanding? Isn't this the same inquiry we have concerning our students? Why don't they study, practice, invest, commit, dedicate, and enjoy the benefits of their efforts?

Humans, by nature, enjoy comfort. In addition to that, we are creatures of habit, and we find ourselves repeating behaviors simply for the sake of fulfilling the requirements of life; in a sense, we do what we do to maintain the status quo or to get to the point of "it's good enough." Therefore, our students replicate the behavior by learning what they need to learn to meet the assigned goals, play/sing the chosen music, or complete the requested objectives; it is rare to find those who overachieve or push themselves beyond the targeted finish line.

Instead of focusing on what motivates the individual (in other words, what it takes to stir one to push beyond the given requirements), perhaps we should look at what is holding the person back? What is it that hinders the forward momentum of our students or us? The world of psychology spotlights two specific areas that impede us in our quest for quality: fear of failure and fear of success.

Fear of failure: It is easy to understand the hesitation to leave oneself vulnerable to failure. We have learned to avoid failure at all costs along with the embarrassing emotional pain that accompanies this dreaded outcome. Instead of seeing failure as a stepping stone to achievement, we often see it as a termination point. However, the most successful people we know have all embraced the concept of failure and, in fact, have even used it as a motivating force to accept, correct, and retry the task at hand. There will never be success without failure; therefore, failure must be reframed in our understanding as part of the formula to help us reach our highest goals and aspirations.

Fear of success: Why would someone be frightened of the prospect of success? Isn't that what we are trying to achieve? Isn't that the pay-off for all of our hard work? Ah yes, but success brings along some companions that are not always part of our comfort zone.

- **More responsibility:** A successful person will be expected to uphold the level of responsibility needed to maintain the achieved standard.

- **Higher expectations:** Winners are expected to keep winning. In most cases this means going beyond the level of the initial success.

- **Being in the limelight:** Successful people are seen and heard by all. There is no place to hide; others are always scrutinizing those who are successful.

- **The long fall to the next failure:** When the successful person faces the inevitable failure, the distance to the bottom of the mountain is greater than it is for those who do not try at all.

- **Separation from friends:** Success often creates a chasm between the individual and the rest of the crowd. Peer pressure often serves as the deciding factor in whether to push the extra mile or not; it is easier to stay with the crowd and play it safe.

Based on the two expressed fears (failure/success), the most comfortable place to be is "it's good enough." The mind logically concludes, "Do what you have to do to avoid failure, but be careful not to catapult yourself to a high level of success."

To counteract this reasoning, we, as educators, must be the first to model the benefits of both failure and success. In other words, we must be willing to set the pace by demonstrating our own willingness to push the envelope of possibility. Failure (resulting from an effort to achieve) needs to be rewarded with guided encouragement to "learn from the mistakes" and then use the newly discovered data as we make a second, third, and fourth attempt. Success (resulting from a calculated effort) needs to be acknowledged immediately, followed by the assurance that the value of the learning process was more important than the achieved product or outcome.

Students will reach beyond "it's good enough" when they understand there are personal benefits to both failure and success; we, as educators, must reinforce this behavior to insure the positive seeking of higher levels of proficiency becomes an integral part of our students' behavior.

The only time "it's good enough" is when we decide to take action on the fact that it's not good enough.

Chapter 6

Worth Our Weight in Goals!

Unless you know to what port you sail,
no wind is a good wind.
Remember, too, that winds change with each day,
and sails are trimmed to meet existing winds.

"There is just never enough time! It seems like I just finish taking roll when the bell rings. The frustration is driving me nuts!"

"Each year I promise myself not to get entangled in this trap of always being behind and never getting caught up, but it just seems to be a pattern I can't break. How do other teachers get everything done?"

"If someone would just tell me one thing I could count on to really help with this situation of too much to do and not enough time to do it in, it would be worth everything to me."

Have you ever heard these statements? Perhaps they have even passed through your lips. They seem to be inherent in the profession, don't they? How does one stay on top of the situation and not fall prey to the anxiety caused by constant incompletion of work?

Goal-setting is nothing revolutionary in the educational world. In fact, we have all memorized the "benefit package" available to the individual who establishes goals. And, most certainly, we all have goals. Our students have goals. Our schools have goals. Everyone has goals. However, in looking a step further, it is evident that successful teachers maintain a serious, disciplined pattern when it comes to short- and long-term goal setting. Their consistently high level of accomplishment serves as a positive testimony to the worth of this process. The exercise does pay off.

Do we carefully plan our day? Specifically design our week of classes? Outline the first and second priority goals of the month, the semester, the year? Or are we flying by the seats of our pants? This is an uncomfortable set of questions, isn't it? How quickly we are reminded of that familiar quote: "Failing to plan means planning to fail."

We will spend hours selecting the "perfect" music for the upcoming concert or planning for an upcoming field trip but will not extend that same detailed preparation to the planning of the rehearsal or class format. Not only is this self-defeating, but it becomes a vicious circle leading to personal stress, poor performances, strained rehearsals, and a constant battle for program survival. These negative results confirm our worst fears and reinforce the subconscious mind. Further, the cycle is certain to repeat itself again (a classic case of self-fulfilling prophecy).

How does one break the cycle? What steps can be taken to alter this seemingly endless, predictable outcome? The answer might well be within the logic of these questions:

- Would you start driving across the country without a map?

- Would you attempt to put together a jigsaw puzzle without the picture on the box?

- Have you ever boarded a plane without knowing its destination?

How ridiculous and simplistic these questions appear! Only a fool would be lured into such nonsense.

Our minds lead us in the direction of their most dominant thoughts. Are we taking control of those thoughts and carefully "mapping out" our futures, or do we simply hope everything will fall in place?

It is imperative that we set the goals—draw our map, define the intent, lay out the plans, create the blueprint—which will determine the success of our efforts.

The mind works on goals like a homing pigeon. Without a destination, the homing pigeon is known to fly in circles until it collapses in a heap of exhaustion. It is time to focus our efforts, just as we would focus a camera before taking a photograph to insure a clean, crisp representation of the vision.

Setting goals—creating our vision in detail—is more than just "thinking through" what the day has in store on our way to school.

Goals must be written. It is a highly skilled procedure with strict rules demanding self-discipline at the highest level.

Goals must be specific. The more detailed we can make the goals, the greater the chance we will reach them. It is mandatory that we write them down and create as many outlined sub-entries as possible.

Goals must be realistic. Aladdin was not a teacher. This routine is futile if we are extreme in either direction: too easy or too difficult. Assess the students' potential, then set the goals one rung higher on the ladder of success.

Goals must match our values. If the results of the goal setting are inconsistent with out values, the mind will wipe out the goals much like a computer will erase a document. The plan must be congruent with our purpose in teaching, our purpose in life, and our purposeful being.

Goals must be visualized in detail. Be able to share the vision with the students in a way they understand, and see the picture. Enthusiasm and positive energy will always be available when they are clearly aware of their destination.

Goals must be measurable. If we cannot measure the goals, we cannot chart the progress. Without progress, there is no positive feedback for the mind, and the energy level subsides. Much like a car without gasoline, the goals are without fuel and fall far short of the mark. This common flaw often prevents people from achieving complete success.

Read and review the goals daily. Each time the message is sent to the mind, it reestablishes the forward momentum. Much as a gyroscope keeps a center to an airplane's flight with constant course corrections, our mind needs to be fed data to adjust where necessary for goal attainment.

It all sounds so easy. It's not! At least at first, it's not. But, like anything else, the habit of doing it time and time again becomes like all other patterns of life. After a given amount of time (twenty-one to twenty-eight days the experts say), goal setting becomes an integral part of our daily routine.

Good planting means a good harvest. Good habits develop good results.

Perhaps it is not the will to do good that counts, but the will to prepare to do good.

We all have the ability for success, but we often allow ourselves to be programmed for failure. After listening to countless people explain why something cannot be accomplished, our subconscious begins to accept this information, and we start to behave accordingly. Personal motivation dwindles, and it becomes impossible to define our goals or even explain our plan for reaching the chosen destination. Much like our friend the homing pigeon, we struggle in a hopeless attempt to break out of this professional entrapment. Such an emotional straitjacket unfortunately often leads to the proverbial burnout syndrome.

It is not a dead-end street. The process of goal setting brings with it an abundance of personal drive. The more vividly we can describe our goals, the more energy is available to us. It has also been demonstrated repeatedly that a disciplined goal-choice will always override a failure-choice in the mind. The choice seems clear!

I recently read a gripping statement of truth that brings all of this to an appropriate end: A person who does not improve is no better than a person who cannot improve.

The goal is to strive for excellence in every facet of our daily lives. Unless we commit to excellence, we are doomed to mediocrity. Why settle for less?

Are we worth our weight in goals?

Chapter 7

The Proof Is in the Pudding

> *A mistake is at least evidence that someone*
> *tried to do something.*

Education is full of little axioms we all pass over somewhere in our education classes in college and soon forget in the midst of the everyday tasks at hand. But they crop up several years later and make more sense now that we have the experiences to understand them. So much of what we teach in leadership workshops is centered on the things we already know but fail to put into practice each day. If we are to succeed at anything when we are dealing with other people, we had better be in command of the laws of leadership. This is one such law: I hear—I forget; I see—I remember; I do—I understand!

I HEAR—I FORGET. It's true! We remember about 10 percent of what we hear. In terms of teaching (leadership), we can quickly see the application of this to any facet of the typical classroom. How many times have we spent countless hours going over the very same material, lecturing until we were blue in the face, only to have a student continue to make the same mistake time and time again? If we are to follow this formula, we would have to say everything ten times to insure that the student (follower) would completely understand. And then, of course, the next time we run into the same problem, we are up for another ten swings at the ball before there is any guarantee of hitting it.

Maybe there is a better way!

I SEE—I REMEMBER. Have you ever watched a group play a concert with their heads buried in the music? On the podium, the conductor is frantically trying to get the attention of the group so he or she can institute some musical interpretation.

The retention rate jumps to 24 percent when the students are watching. Simply by keeping the eyes on a teacher, the students will retain an additional 14 percent. So, in any form of communication, it is a necessity to make eye contact with those around you. Never give instructions without making sure the students (followers) are watching you. Demand and command eye contact.

Maybe there is a better way!

I DO—I UNDERSTAND! Ah, yes! When we participate in anything, our level of retention jumps to 80 percent. If you truly want those you are leading to grasp any concept, you must get them to do it! A more pragmatic way of saying this is: Quit talking so much! Quit demonstrating so much! Have the person do it more! Experience is always the best teacher in the world.

What does this have to do with leadership?

When we pass out the assignments for various leadership roles, the instructions often stop there. We assume the person is going to be able to deal with his or her peers. That is rarely the case. Thus, much time is wasted as these leaders go about telling their followers what to do (10 percent retention), showing them what to do by doing it themselves as a demonstrator (24 percent retention), and having the followers (learners) actually doing the task for a very short time (80 percent retention). And, as we all know, the success of any leader is in direct proportion to their ability to produce excellence in the people they are leading.

Now, if you want your leaders to benefit from this article, don't read it to them, and don't put it on the board for them to read, but sit down with them and go over it together. Make a list of "to do's" that will improve their performance in the class and then have the class complete them.

Let's not talk about creating excellence or observing those who have created excellence, but let's go about creating excellence. Real leadership comes out of action. The proof is in the pudding! Take some action!

Chapter 8

Student Behavior: Fact, Not Fiction

There are no limits to the amount of good you can accomplish if you don't care who gets the credit.

Teacher? Psychologist? Counselor? Performer? Confidant? And other assorted job-related responsibilities included in the profession!

How many psychology courses did you take in college? Do you ever feel you're facing a problem with a student that is beyond your expertise in relationship to counseling or guidance for the student's well being? Is most of your time spent teaching, or do you find yourself spending all of your time handling various situations within the environment just to keep the program afloat?

We are never totally prepared for what faces us as teachers, and when we are confronted with the reality of the educational world, it can be a frightening, frustrating, confusing, and discouraging set of experiences. Many things you are asked to do as an educator are well beyond your expertise (i.e., disciplinary action, emotional unrest). The instinctive behavior is to scream, "foul!" The truth is, right or wrong, prepared or not prepared, you will face such circumstances. So rather than waste nonproductive energy on whether it's "fair" or not, let's assume a positive posture and begin to seek information on how to deal with the problems at hand. Act instead of react, and shift from merely existing to creative growth, where we can examine and solve problems.

Nice words, but how does this ideological fairyland become a reality? To begin with, we must acknowledge some of the things going on for young people in today's teenage world. You may not like all of this data, but to dismiss it is setting yourself up for certain failure in your teaching career. When we understand and learn about the behavior patterns of youths, then (and only then) can we begin to work with them, not in spite of them.

Do you remember you first real day of teaching? How excited you were to impart all of your knowledge into those thirsty little minds! Remember your visions of all the students waiting in eager anticipation of every word of wisdom you were going to share with them? More fairyland. Rarely does it happen that way, or even come close to it because we have been working under the false assumption that the students will be filled with a tremendous desire to learn, a dangerous as well as inaccurate deduction. Successful teachers are those people who accept the reality of the situation at hand and move forward from that point. They have a grip on where the students are coming from and are assertive in the necessity to go to them instead of waiting for the students to magically "come of age."

We all need to see that teenagers are facing a higher degree of stress than ever before. Their lives are full of pressures that not only dictate their daily behavior, but cause them to make choices in need of adult counterbalance. Whether we agree about our own need to handle this added responsibility (on the teacher's part) isn't the questions. You will handle it; you have no choice. How to handle it is the question. Any music teacher would agree that playing in tune is important, but if the child behind the instrument is dealing with a broken home, extended pressure to make grades to qualify for a certain college, drug or alcohol abuse, emotional crises with friends, trying to work and go to school at the same time, etc., you can correct the technical part of the problem, but you still have the problem. Next time out-of-tune note appears, guess what?!

Too often, we react to this particular situation by overreacting. Venting anger, embarrassing the student, espousing "Lecture 26" to the entire group, or whatever, will not solve the problem. The problem is that the student is so preoccupied with a stressful situation (regardless of when it happened) that he or she isn't even aware of the out-of-tune note. Sometimes the student isn't even in the room, so to speak. The immediate, and all-too-common response is, "Well, they shouldn't drag their feelings into the class and ruin it for everyone else!" None of us should! But we do, and we must deal with what is, not what should be.

The teenage world has become a microcosm of the adult world, and the trend of growing up quickly has brought with it all the emotional hazards and ailments of the adult world. We simply can't ignore these issues; they are real, and we must adjust our teaching techniques to deal with them, or the play-ing will never be in tune...nor will the students...nor will you!

What can I do? How can I help? In what direction do I go?

Once we begin to face the situation with a clear understanding, we have won half the battle. Sidestepping the issues simply adds fuel to the present fire. If you've made it this far in the article, you have taken a big step. The following suggestions will serve as guidelines. There is no answer that will solve every problem because every problem is unique to that situation. This information will give you some idea of where your energy will be best spent.

Don't try to turn the clock back. Too many people want to return to the "good old days." While they are verbalizing about how great things used to be, the excellent teachers are dealing with the present and preparing for the future. Update!

Express your care for students by saying no! Young people need help in decision making. Teach the value of giving up the short-term instant gratification in exchange for the long-term goal...and teach that the enjoyment comes via the journey, or focus. Learning to deal with "no" can be the most meaningful tool you share with them.

In every decision, deal with the principle, not the pressure. Young people have learned the game of manipulation very well from the adult world, and you can easily get conned into doing something in complete opposition to what would be most beneficial to the program. When the students understand your thinking is always based on what is best for them in the overall scheme of things, they will begin to respect your decision-making. You must be honest with your own integrity. You won't always be popular, but you will be a great role model for everyone!

Teach persistence by being persistent. Learning by example is still the most effective method. If your students observe you tackling the problems of the day with a positive approach, they are likely to copy or mirror your behavior when they are around you. Beware: the reverse of this is also true when applied to negative example. A great friend once told me he could predict the performance of any group by spending ten minutes with the director in his or her office. His theory was amazingly accurate. Persistence is an absolute must in growth. Demonstrate how to stretch and grow through expanding your limits. Be an effective mirror source.

Deal with the confronting issues immediately and privately. Although discipline problems and irritating happenings invite the intimidation "sledgehammer," the "instant resolution" technique will come back to haunt you. Whenever we embarrass someone into behaving or seeing it our way, the problem will silently snowball and appear with much more intensity than the original issue. Get it out in the open and clean it up!

Encourage communication at all levels. When you find some divisions in the organization and a "coldness" about individuals, sections, or various groups sets in, it is much like the calm before the storm. The only way to offset the problem is with communication. Share what is going on with your students, your colleagues, your administration—everyone who touches your life. Communication is a learned habit, and it must be practiced. Set the example!

Be calm and logical. Students are looking for some stability. Because of the extreme emotions that make up a good part of teenage growth patterns (the do-or-die situations) it is so important they have an offsetting personality. This counterbalance in life could be your most important contribution to their lives.

Have a sense of humor—lighten up! Too often, we extend far too much anxiety toward a problem. Take care of it, and move on. Learn to be "glad" right after you're "mad." Stick to your guns, and don't let any negative emotion drag through an entire day. Only in traumatic experiences does trauma have any real value. Teenagers need to see that life doesn't have to be lived at the emotional pace of their favorite soap opera.

Now, let's return to square one.

None of us took enough psychology courses to give us all the answers. The answers lie within the personal research we do each day.

If you feel inadequate about handling some of the student's emotional upset, welcome aboard! Simply take it one step at a time, and express care every step of the way. There is no use straightening the lampshade if the house is burning down!

Chapter 9

The Solution to Success Is in the Mirror

The credit belongs to the man who is actually in the arena; whose face is marred by dust and sweat and blood; who strives valiantly; who errs and comes short again and again... who knows the great enthusiasms, the great devotion, and spends himself in a worthy cause; who at the best knows in the end the triumph of high achievement; and who at the worst, if he fails, at least fails while daring greatly.

—Theodore Roosevelt

When a program is failing, it appears everyone is to blame (the students, parents, administrators, and members of the community) for the bleak circumstances. If that is so, it is time for some positive influence from an enthusiastic leader who refuses to accept the conditions as they are, but is committed to infusing life into the program and offering hope to everyone who eagerly seeks a pathway to success. Who could that savior be? Who is willing to go that extra mile?

The answer is quite simple: it is the person we see when we look in the mirror. There is the solution to the problem! The question is: are we willing to pay the price? It means breaking old habits and developing new patterns that will allow us to generate the effect, rather than be "at the effect." We will have to take the road less traveled, and the journey can be very long and very lonely, but it leads to success— success for everyone who wants to be a part of excellence.

Unfortunately, we have become masters of blame. Every time something does not meet our expectations, we tend to blame someone or something. However, whenever we blame, we give up our power over the situation. We have, in fact, given in to the circumstances and have allowed the situation to determine our reaction instead of our pro-action to determine the situation. This certain pathway to failure is so subtle that most of us don't realize we are on it. What's more, we will defend why we had to blame someone or something, which is just another coating of blame! How paradoxical!

The powerful human mind will always be right; therefore, whatever we see as true in effect becomes true (self-fulfilling prophecy). The only way out of this downward spiral is to change (reprogram) our minds to believe it can work. At the very moment of the acceptance of the new belief, we begin to refocus on the various aspects of the situation that prove us right, but this time we are right about the belief that things will be taking a turn for the better, and, once again, we are confirmed: it will work.

Too simplistic, you say. (That's just more "being right" about the fact that it won't work, and everything continues in the predictable old negative pattern. The mind wins, you lose. It's frustrating, isn't it? This is exactly what got us in this predicament in the first place.) If we want to shift this and upgrade to a new level of living, we must leave the comfort zone and risk some new thoughts, new ideas, and even new experiences with an entirely new attitude.

Leaving our comfort zone is frightening. This fear will often serve as a barrier to keep us from taking that all-important step to a new understanding. We become sarcastic, cynical, and even hostile about those who challenge us to break away from those comfortable habits. It's not that we are satisfied; rather, we are afraid of what might be a waiting us in the unknown parts of life. As one person told me, "No, I don't want to change. I'm not really satisfied with my life, but if I gamble and make these personal changes, things might get worse than they already are, so it is just easier to stay where I am. At least I know how to handle life at this level." Is that living or just maintenance? Is that a positive role model for our students' attitudes?

On the other hand, there are many people who are exploring life at its fullest. They have learned to use fear as their ally and turn the energy of fear (which often holds us back) into the energy of risk and continue to add to their library of experiences by learning, growing, discovering, and enjoying the full range of dynamics in living.

Which person would you predict would be the most effective teacher? Which one would inspire the students to jump headfirst into their studies? Which one would you like to be around if you were a student?

Which of these people do you see when you look in the mirror?

It is often uncomfortable to discuss being uncomfortable. These kinds of articles are not popular because they challenge each of us (including me) to come out of ourselves and reveal our insecurities. We are vulnerable and often defenseless, so the constant temptation is to run back inside our safe character and avoid any chance of the embarrassment of failure. (How ironic that this process assures failure and even is failure!) The only real security is to admit that we are insecure, just as the only real competence is to admit that we are incompetent. When we are willing to bring this truth forward and embrace it, we begin to empower ourselves and do not have to resort to blame. We can use that energy to start to take action to improve the conditions. What lies behind us and what lies ahead of us is pale compared to what lies within us. The answer is in the mirror!

The many cultures of the world have brought forth some remarkable wisdom. The following story, an ancient Hindu legend, is one that provokes a great deal of thought in a gently humorous way. Please understand it is not a religious message or an implication of suggested metaphysical beliefs, but a chance to understand the tremendous potential we all have.

At one time, all men on earth were gods. But they so sinned and abused the Divine, that Brahma, the god of all gods, decided that the power of the godhead should be taken away from man and hidden someplace where man would never find it and abuse it again.

"We will bury it deep in the earth," said the other gods.

"No," said Brahma, "because man will dig down in the earth and find it."

"Then we will sink it into the deepest ocean," they said.

"No," said Brahma, "because man will learn to dive and find it there too."

"We will hide it on the highest mountain," they said.

"No," said Brahma, "because man will some day climb every mountain on the earth and again capture the godhead."

"Then where can we hide it where man cannot find it?" asked the lesser gods.

"I will tell you," said Brahma, "hide it down in man himself. He will never think to look there."

Ah, yes. We are once again reminded through this fable that the solution to success is in the mirror.

Chapter 10

Cooperation Creates Victory

Together we stand, divided we fall.

We are a society that thrives on competition. We compete in school for grades; we compete in our professional lives to achieve positions and titles; and we compete in our daily life patterns for everything from a faster lane on the freeway to a winning number in the local lottery. We like to win, to get ahead, to maneuver ourselves to a better vantage point. Perhaps Darwin's proposed theory in his popular writing *The Origin of the Species* clearly evidences our competitive spirit, our ongoing, ever-present striving to get to the front of the pack. It is powerful motivational fuel for humans, but like any energy force, competition can be used in a positive or negative fashion.

Observing the positive enthusiasm generated by competition in athletics, other disciplines have quickly jumped on the bandwagon. Our schools now have science fairs, 4-H shows, debate clubs, essay contests, and music festivals recognizing the achievements of an array of talents ranging from a flute solo to a 400-piece marching band.

The good news is all of these organized competitive forums have created much excitement; however, we must be clearly aware that there can be a down side to the win-at-all-costs attitude. As educators, the cautionary responsibility rests directly on our shoulders. Take heed, for the instant gratification of first place can become a haunting detriment when it alone is the only measure of accomplishment.

When we ask students to "go the extra mile" by committing their valuable time to learning, we must focus on the intrinsic benefits they will gain as a result of their investment, rather than the extrinsic rewards that come as a by-product of their dedication. If "getting first place" is more important than the joy of an inspired performance (whatever the adjudication outcome) then it is time to do some philosophical prioritizing. Is the goal to add more trophies of achievement to the shelves in the front lobby or to stretch the students to a new level of communication? The growth of the students must stand as the top priority in every instance.

Over the years, the ongoing debate about the value of competition has caused many educators to avoid any aspect of adjudication/evaluation. Much like the ostrich with its head in the sand, this may be an overreaction or escape; it may also be an unrealistic approach to preparing our students to address the realities of life. At the same time, if everything is couched in a competitive framework, the need to beat the fellow student takes precedence over the personal growth and development gained by a solid program of healthy self-discipline. The key to a successful balance is achieved through the careful guidance of the teacher. Instead of dangling the proverbial competitive carrot in front of the students, we might be better served if we rewarded and recognized their successful habits and patterns.

For example:

1. **Resolving a problem.** Many students are quick to recognize or identify problems, but there are few who will come up with a resolution. Those who do should be

put in the spotlight and given responsibilities within the program.

2. **Making decisions and taking action.** There are many who "wait to be told what to do," then do it remarkably well. Look for those who go one step beyond and are willing to take a stand, make a choice, and follow-through on their decisions; herein lie the leaders of tomorrow.

3. **Loyalty.** In today's world, loyalty is a treasured attribute. Competition is the test of one's loyalty, not when we win, but when we lose. To avoid the "If we can't win, I quit!" attitude, reinforce the character strength of loyalty.

4. **Cooperation.** Nothing is impossible when a group of individuals chooses to make cooperation the theme of the working atmosphere. Alternately, it is almost impossible to move any group forward when they are constantly competing to gain the upper hand on their fellow students.

It is apparent that we needn't beat another person or persons to win; we simply need to improve ourselves to experience the intrinsic victory that is a result of learning, growing, and becoming. To this end, let us continue to support one another and realize the value of competition is merely a stepping stone for our students to witness others who share a similar passion. When all is said and done, we must band together if we ever hope to attain true victory.

Chapter 11

Creating a Positive Learning Atmosphere

> *One difference between savagery and civilization is a little courtesy. There's no telling what a lot of courtesy would do.*
> **—Cullen Hightower**

As teachers, we all have a desire to present valuable information to our students. We want them to understand the importance and the impact of our presentation. There is a desire to leave every class with a sense of personal accomplishment and the feeling that we presented the students with data that will better their lives.

Unfortunately, that isn't always the case, is it? As an educator, what is your greatest frustration? Is it the crowded schedule? The required curriculum? The lack of facilities? The inadequate equipment? The poor financial support? Although all of these issues may bring about some anxiety, it seems that most teachers are concerned about the students' comprehension of the material presented.

Did they "get it"?

Did they learn how to integrate the subject matter into their daily patterns? Can they draw upon this knowledge to improve their understanding of the subject? There is often a huge gap between the teacher's presentation and the students' perception of the material shared. How can we bridge that chasm and end the mutual student/teacher frustration?

Communication is not what we say, but what they get. Simply standing in front of a class and offering information is not teaching. The teaching process only happens when there is an exchange. Much like a computer modem, before there can be any transfer of material both the transmitter and the receiver must be operative, using the same language, and programmed to accept this process. If either computer is not properly set up, it will be an unsuccessful venture. (Those of you who have explored the high-tech world are well aware of the frustration when the process does not work!) The teaching/learning endeavor is much the same: both parties must be in the right mode if there is going to be the needed delivery and reception of the lesson(s).

When the computer transaction fails, we review the instructions and try again. If we still are not getting results, we call someone who knows about computer modems. When all else fails, we dial that magic "tech support" number and have an expert talk us through the procedure. In other words, we don't give up until we have accomplished our goal. If nothing else, it is a good lesson in persistence and tenacity. The computer simply will not settle for less than "the right way," and it doesn't care if we are frustrated or not; the computer demands we be correct before it will accept our instructions. We can abuse it, confuse it, refuse it (and even threaten to lose it!), but it stoically sits there on the desk and awaits the input of the proper commands. (Computers are the master teachers of patience.)

Students are far less resilient and far less demanding, and we are never quite sure if they really understand. It is much easier to "give up" on the student than it is on the computer. Even if they do not comprehend the material we present, we can always say they didn't fulfill their learning responsibility. Can you envision saying that to a computer? It's pointless, isn't it?

If positive learning is to occur, it requires a two-step process:

1. The student must be mentally programmed and ready to accept the material.

2. The data must be worthwhile and have substantive value.

It seems so simple, doesn't it? Any credible teacher will make certain that the lesson plan is built upon solid information. The second step of the equation is a direct reflection of our own study, planning, and continued research. However, if we dwell only on this facet of the formula, we will be unsuccessful. If the student is not in the receive mode, the transmission of material will be futile.

With that in mind, let us look carefully at the problem that faces many of us: how do we get the students to want to learn? Noted educational psychologist Stephen Glenn says that when students are in an environment where they are encouraged to risk (and often fail), they are much more eager to become involved in the learning process. Failure is not something to be concerned about but becomes another stepping stone in the journey of goal attainment. However, if their failure results in reprimands, shame, guilt, pain, or blame, they quickly learn to take the path of least resistance and begin practicing self-defense rather than focusing their energies on learning. Once the walls of self-protection go up, there is little chance that new information can get to the student. You could well give the finest lesson in the history of humankind, but unless the student is ready, all is lost.

As teachers, when we address a student (or anyone), we must be certain we do not threaten their egos or violate their human dignity. This does not mean that we simply sit back and avoid any sense of discipline—quite the contrary. There can be no learning without discipline, but we must be wise in the way we create and sustain a healthy learning atmosphere.

When things are going awry, we often take the shortcut by addressing the character of the student rather than the inappropriateness of the behavior. This appears to be a solid solution, for it usually gets the student (as well as the rest of the class) to focus, and the behavior problems seem to disappear, at least momentarily. However, the student goes through the mental processes of resentment, revenge, and retreat. In most cases, the third option, retreat, is the best choice. They sit in class, well behaved, quietly going through the motions, and learning nothing.

If we substitute encouragement for criticism or praise, we then offer that same student the chance to fail, and immediately they try again, and again, and again, until they master the assigned material. They understand we are not going to judge their performances, but join them in the process of learning. The student, in turn, becomes encouraged (in the presence of courage) and their acceptance of our advice becomes much greater. They realize we are allies in the process and not threats to their egos or their dignity. We merely adjust their behavior so they can benefit from their efforts.

Part one of our successful teaching formula is now in place.

There is one major flaw in the analogy between a computer modem and student learning. We can become very frustrated with the computer and unload our wrath on its emotionless screen and storm out of the room in a fit of anxious frustration, but when we come back, the computer will forgive us and we can pick up right where we left off.

That is not the case with students. They remember. They carry the scars of our outbursts with them for a lifetime. Their sense of trust is damaged. They hurt...and often want to hurt us back. The computer doesn't care; the human does, and that's what makes us human.

Do you know any computers that can sing or play an instrument without being humanly manipulated? I don't.

Perhaps the frustrations we experience as teachers should be the schedules, the curricula, the equipment, etc. It should not be the students, for they represent the ultimate in human potential. They are the thinkers, feelers, and doers. Unlike a computer, they do not have a set amount of memory. They are limitless.

Every day, we should be challenged to create an environment that is conducive to risk and failure so each student will be safe and secure in the learning process rather than retreating to a comfort zone where survival becomes a higher priority than personal growth.

Part Two:
Developing an Attitude for Success

Chapter 12

Achieving Excellence

*Where I was is destroyed,
where I am stands condemned,
where I shall be is just now being built.*

When we all have the potential to succeed at almost anything we choose, why do so few people attain a high level accomplishment? What do the top achievers know that others do not? What habits do the successful individuals bring to their life patterns that ensure their attainment of personal and professional goals?

It has been said we use only 6 percent of our mind power, and the latest research shows it may only be 2 percent for normal daily behavior. We are like powerful computers with no instruction manual for success. The great minds of past and present may not have been as great as we all thought, but were merely men and women wise enough to delve into their untapped potential and uncover a limitless supply of possibilities. What was it they discovered? What is the key that unlocks our otherwise dormant abilities? How do we master this technique?

The concept of self-fulfilling prophecy is one that every one of us must deal with in our quest for excellence. In truth, we get what we expect. We never do better than we think we can. The pictures and visions we place in our minds influence our lives.

There have been countless Pygmalion experiments over the years all yielding the same result: If we can change the self-concept of the individual, the behavior results will match. We become who we think we are.

The implications of this understanding in the world of education are far-reaching. If we know, for the most part, that students will not perform beyond our expectation levels, then we also know the same is true of us. Are we constantly learning and grooming ourselves to be the best we can be, or have we opted to fall into the comfortable trap of "it's good enough?"

Do we see ourselves as producing a high-quality environment where we can constantly improve the understanding and performance of our students, or are we simply glad just to get through the day, week, month, and year? In short, do we hold high expectations for ourselves knowing it will determine the success of our classes?

These can be very uncomfortable questions, for they confront the very foundation of our values as teachers who effectively bring new insights to our students so they will live more prosperous lives. At the same time, they offer us an opportunity to take an inventory of our present situation and either move forward or make necessary adjustments according to the findings.

Success is not an accident. It is a predictable pattern and, like any good, tested formula, it works when the individual works. In many cases, the price of success is doing what others don't want to do, or going the extra mile when others have chosen to give up.

If it is so easy, why don't more people participate? Why do most people live far below their potentials? The number one reason: the inability to delay gratification.

Many are tempted to choose fun and easy over difficult and necessary, or tension relieving over goal achieving. We know that bad habits are easy to form but hard to live with, while good habits are hard to form but easy to live with. The obvious choice is to create positive habits that avoid the quick fix and offer long-range benefits. Every self-improvement program, from Weight Watchers to time management, is useless without this fundamental ingredient: the personal belief and self-discipline needed to delay gratification until the envisioned goal is attained. Once this is in place, the journey begins. Even after arrival, the next step is a wise maintenance program that continues the process in the future.

Where does one start? What is the first step? Is this just more mumbo-jumbo, or can it really work for me?

Different programs work for different people. However, every success story has one common theme: the commitment of the individual to see it through to the end. A half-hearted effort produces half-hearted results.

The following guidelines serve as a launchpad:

1. **Set clearly defined goals.** There is little or no personal motivation without goals. The more detailed and defined the goals, the more energy you will produce to reach them. So often, goals are too general: "I want to be happy." "I want to be successful." "My goal is to have people respect me."

   These are admirable, but goal-setting needs to be specific. Use calendar dates as goal markers. Create personal deadlines. Make certain the goals are measurable and attainable, and be certain to write them down. They serve as your road map to success. Perhaps one of your goals would be to learn how to set goals. It is a very exciting process, but it takes delayed gratification to accomplish the task.

2. **Commit to your area of excellence.** Unless we commit to excellence, we are doomed to mediocrity. Throw yourself

into the pursuit of excellence. Spend time studying and learning everything you can about your chosen area of expertise. Beware of complacency. Surround yourself with others who have a like interest and passion and support this mutual interest. Rekindle the childhood enthusiasm that offers direction to inquisition. Become an expert in some facet of life and invite those around you to participate and enjoy the benefits of learning and growing toward a higher level of competence.

3. **Review your goals and measure your daily progress.** Out of sight, out of mind. Remember that the mind leads us in the direction of its most dominant thought. The positive effects of "self-talk" are well known to those who practice the art of visioning. See yourself achieving the intended short-range and long-range goals. Keep your success-pictures at the forefront of your conscious mind. Much unhappiness comes from not knowing one's destination; therefore, constantly remind yourself of how far you've come and where you still need to go. Build on what you know. Success builds success. Be faithful to your master plan. Treat it as you would the most important thesis assignment of your career: it could well be.

4. **Stay on task: persistance is self-discipline in action.** If you want to increase your success rate, increase your failure rate. There will be adversity; accept it, even embrace it. Every time you meet a situation that slows your progress, ask yourself, "What is there for me to learn?" Within the problem is certain to be the clue for the next forward move.

Unfortunately, it is popular to quit after so many false starts or thwarted efforts. In the classic words of

Winston Churchill (who repeated a grade in school, by the way): "Never give up. Never, never give up." Where would the world be today if Sir Winston would have chosen to quit after his educational setback? Every breakthrough in our modern world is a result of some persistent (and often stubborn) person who refused to accept defeat. There is no substitute for fulfilled commitment. It is the primary fuel for a healthy self-esteem.

5. **Accept total responsibility.** See yourself as the cause, not the effect. This simple premise offers a very strong personal power base for motivation. When something goes awry, accept the responsibility and avoid the temptation to blame someone. Blame gets us "off the hook," but it also violates our responsibility factor. Focus on solutions, not problems. Count on yourself to come through in every situation. Pay the price, and pay it in advance. This is where delayed gratification is put to the test. The more responsible we are, the better we like ourselves.

6. **Acknowledge your supporting cast.** Dynamic people have the ability to uplift the spirits of those around them. Your personal health is in direct proportion to your ability to get along with others. Let other people know and understand your goals so they can support you in the effort. You can't go at it alone. Eventually you are going to need someone's help, expertise, direction, or whatever. Everyone likes to be around a successful person, so share the glory of the victory with all those who played a role in your accomplishment. You will quickly discover an eager group of people awaiting the opportunity to work with you in the future.

A person with clear, focused goals will outstrip a genius every time. Success awaits us all. Will we take the road less traveled? The game of self-discipline takes lifelong study, practice, and discipline. It may not be the "will to succeed" that counts as much as the "will to prepare to succeed." The above six-step formula is a preparation course aimed at achieving success. Once we have reached the summit of this mountain (goal), we quickly see other mountains (goals) that require further self-discipline.

A more simplistic approach came from a friend who has enjoyed success throughout his life. I asked him one day, "To what do you attribute all your many accomplishments in life?" He smiled and said quietly, "I found out what unsuccessful people do, and I don't do it."

Enough said.

Chapter 13

The Price of Success

Happiness...lies in the joy
of achievement,
in the thrill of creative effort.
—Franklin D. Roosevelt

To date, I have not met anyone who did not want to be successful in whatever he or she chose. Not many say, "I think I'll just be mediocre...it seems to satisfy my needs!" Yet there are people who seem to avoid success because of rather meaningless, shallow excuses. Why? Why would anyone settle for less than he or she can be? As teachers, do we not all have the obligation to serve as role models of and for excellence?

Is it that people don't want to be successful, or is it that we have not learned how to be successful? We certainly have an abundance of information, which should "boost us to the top." However, there are still countless examples of people who are not willing to take the risk of going for it. Yes, that includes both you and me.

What would you do if you knew there was no way you could fail?

Isn't that fun to think about? If you knew there was no way you could lose, be side-tracked, detoured, embarrassed, humiliated, or intimidated. If you knew you would forfeit nothing, but only gain and benefit, what would you do? Isn't it true that most of us have set limits on what we can do simply through self-inflicted barriers? Literally, our success is our own doing. We have the potential to do just about anything (and it may well be anything!) we choose. Yes, we do! To say, "Nah, we don't," is just more self-limitation. It is a matter of convincing ourselves (our self-image) that we are capable of going beyond our present-day limits.

In a brilliant analogy, author Anthony Robbins explains the way our mind works on electronic impulses (based on research done at Stanford University). We can now identify the positive and negative impulses being sent via brain waves, which dictate our behavior. Negative impulses cause negative behavior, and positive impulses cause positive behavior. The mind, much like a computer, simply processes the message and kicks back the behavioral patterns we are to act out. The mind cannot distinguish whether they are right or wrong, but merely acts upon the given data just as a computer would run whatever disk we insert. The really exciting part is: our conscious mind has the ability to make the choice of what message we want to send! In other words, we choose the program for our own behavioral computer.

When we don't consciously make this choice, the mind will simply take whatever is the loudest sensory information and use it as the computer program. It is like drifting aimlessly at sea, when we have the ability to guide our ship if we take the responsibility of steering it.

There is a "price to pay" for success, just as there is a price to pay for negative conditions. It is not a random "luck of the draw," but a systematic, self-disciplined plan of action that affords everyone the same opportunities for reaching his or her goals.

Not to over-simplify this formula (the reader can rest assured there are volumes written on the subject that warrant study) but the condensation of everything boils down to this three-step process: vision, commitment, action—or for those of us who understand "plain old language"—ready, aim, fire.

VISION (READY)—The people who "make it" have this in common. They see, dream, and envision their goal before it ever becomes reality. They burn it into their sub-conscious and can describe every detail of their dream.

Knowing the mind will always lead us in the direction of our most dominant thought, these winners make sure they are constantly reaching into their creative mind to shape/sculpt/draw their exact blueprint of the future. They leave nothing to chance.

COMMITMENT (AIM)—Successful people understand that "the world is not devoted to making them happy" and face the responsibilities of successful living, knowing it will mean sacrifice in certain areas. But they also understand the personal growth and strength that will result from this effort, which really makes it a benefit.

Anyone can succeed if they are willing to make a personal commitment to handle:

1. FRUSTRATION—Everyone experiences this throughout life.

2. REJECTION—Have you ever met a successful person who has not been subjected to rejection...lots of rejection? In fact, the really successful man or woman sees rejection as a chance to learn and grow.

3. FINANCIAL PRESSURE—Whether we like it or not, it is part of our society. The only certain way not to have any financial pressure is to not have any finances...and that, in itself, could be real pressure!

4. LACK OF WILL TO GROW—Complacency is a dangerous mood. It can cause the mind to rationalize everything from boredom to apathy. When skepticism appears, the "red flag of danger" should be bright in your vision. When we're convinced that "we can't," we become our worst enemies on the road to success.

You must "take aim" through your personal commitment to follow through no matter what obstacles or barriers you encounter. Each disappointment can serve as a stepping stone in reaching the goal.

ACTION (FIRE!)—The last key element of the trilogy. It is easy to "dream the dream" and even exciting to sit down and "draw up the plan," but doing it, actually taking action, seems to be where many halt. If we are expecting people to come to us to support our endeavors, then we have missed the point. If your dream is not worth self-action, what is its value to begin with?

"But what if I miss the target when I fire?" Reload and fire again! "But what if I run out of ammunition?" The fuel to fire your efforts is self-created, and the closer you get to the goal, the more enthusiasm and excitement you will experience. Positive energy produces more positive energy (part of the Stanford research findings) just as negative energy produces negative energy. What is the basis of your energy source? Positive or negative?

It is important to see the order of the system: vision, commitment, action (ready, aim, fire!). If this order is violated, the formula loses its potency, and we all have examples of this in our lives. Don't you know many situations where you have seen something like this: ready, fire, aim. (It is important to have "aim/commitment" in place prior to firing. We might wound someone, including ourselves, by not having a good plan!)

Then there is the case of the over-planner with this common pattern: ready, aim, aim, aim, aim, aim... (These people do not want to "fire/take action" because they don't want that next level of responsibility.)

One of my favorites (self-recognition!) is the infamous: fire, ready, fire, aim, fire! (How many times have we all just wasted human energy in our fruitless attempts to get the job done! No plan, no vision, no goals, no organization, just blind, uncontrolled energy being shot in a hapless, hopeless attempt to hit some unseen target!)

We can all play with the pattern and apply it to any situation. Humor is a catalyst that allows us to understand our errors. If we do not learn from them, we have destroyed the greatest worth of the experience.

The three-part formula is tried and true. It works. Use it!

Success (whatever it is for you, and it is different for all of us) is available in abundance to each of us in our daily work, personal lives, and missions in life. Our limits are exactly that: our limits! Using the "ready, aim, fire" technique for success seems like a small price to pay for making our dreams come true. Just take ten minutes out of your busy day to check yourself. Do you have your vision clearly in mind? Have you carefully established your committed plan of time and organization to get there? Are you taking action to achieve your goals?

What you will gain personally is exciting, but far more important, you will be a role model of endless, limitless possibilities to your students! Let them buy into your success.

That's a price tag every student can afford and will certainly want to purchase! It's a cheap price to pay for personal happiness.

FIRE!

Chapter 14

Dealing with Feelings of Insecurity

*Courage is resistance to fear, mastery of
fear—not absence of fear*
—Mark Twain

When there is any conflict between or among people, it generally stems from a kind of behavior that "turns off" someone else. (Adults label it a personality conflict, which is simply a fancy title describing a situation in which two or more people don't agree.) Often, the term insecure is used as the reason for certain behaviors. "He acts like that because he is insecure." "She talks about other people because she is insecure about herself." "John isn't going to try out for drum major because he feels very insecure about his chances."

The truth is we are all insecure. We can't be experts on everything, and each day of our lives we are faced with problems that involve taking some risks to solve them so we can move on. (Of course, when we risk, we also set ourselves up for failure—and many people simply cannot face failure.) Therefore, if we understand our own insecurities and how we treat them, it will allow us to see why other people behave as they do, and, through this understanding, we can effectively eliminate most (if not all) personality conflicts. Who wouldn't want that? Let's see how people deal with these common feelings and how we can learn to use them to our advantage.

There are six basic reactions to feelings of insecurity. As they are described, you will probably be able to recognize someone in your classroom who fits into this category. The important thing is that we learn to positively use the information to help the person grow.

Withdrawal. Individuals who react to insecurity through withdrawal simply hide within a shell of silence. They will never volunteer to step forward on any project. They are living in constant fear of being picked out of the crowd. (The thought of embarrassment is unbearable.)

To communicate effectively with these individuals, be very gentle in your approach. Harshness and criticism will drive them further back into their shells to the point that they may eventually drop the class rather that face the fear of failing.

Agressive sarcasm. We all recognize the person who always has to make a comment and put others down. The only way the individual can make him- or herself look good is by making others look bad.

The most productive way to deal with this kind of insecurity is to communicate with this person on a one-on-one basis. Never deal with the aggressiveness in front of the group. It only reinforces this behavior as an attention-getter and does nothing to curb the insecurity.

Silliness. Do you have a class clown? This person has to make a joke about everything and is always good for a laugh, even in the most serious moments.

A "true friend" will address the clown and let him or her know the humor is appreciated, but it is not necessary to insure the person's worth. In other words, there is a time and place for everything. (Remember, some people laugh to keep from crying or act silly in order to avoid painful seriousness.)

Indifference. These people are the few who never seem to care about anything. They don't have moments of joy or sadness—they just go through the motions, never demonstrating any readable emotions.

These are very difficult individuals to understand because there appears to be nothing to discuss. Often this reaction of indifference is a result of being hurt in a past experience, so these people feel that if they don't care, then they won't be hurt. Unfortunately this behavior is self-destructive and keeps the individual from enjoying the class. Patience is of primary importance in handling this individual. Take your time. Progress will be slow.

Conformity. Here we have the people who stay in the middle of the road on everything. If everyone else votes yes, they will vote yes also—even if they disagree with the concept. These people focus all their energy on not being different. They feel as long as they are in the middle of the pack, nobody will pick them out, and they won't have to confront their insecurity.

We must remind these people that they are easy prey for everyone. (As long as we have huge numbers in this category, fads will reign supreme, and people will devote their efforts to being just like everyone else instead of themselves.) Usually you can reason with these people; unfortunately, their understanding may be just another form of conformity. Lots of time and energy is necessary here!

Compensation. Here is the person who recognizes the insecurity and decides to do something about it, rather than choose one of the other five non-productive options. These people have the same fears, the same considerations, the same feelings of failure, and the same desires to quit that anyone else may have. The difference is, they don't quit. Instead, they risk, knowing that every success usually has six to eight failures as a prior investment.

How many times have you heard the clever little sayings such as "No pain, no gain" or "When the going gets tough, the tough get going." The truth is these all describe the compensator, the individual who realizes a weakness and goes about solving it through study, practice, extra hours, volunteer duty, courtesy, and lots of blood, sweat, and tears.

A very wise young lady put it quite simply in one of my workshops. She said, "The only difference between a successful person and one who is not is the successful person decides to go for it in spite of their fears." Profound!

As you head into tomorrow, how are you going to deal with your sense of insecurity? Perhaps the most helpful thing we can all do is join together in helping one another conquer our fears and support those around us in taking the risk, by being the first ones on hand to help them if they fail.

We quickly see insecurity is a given in this thing called growing. The choice of how we deal with it is the key to our success.

Chapter 15

Getting Serious about Being Positive

You can't do everything,
but you can do something.

The title of this article should provoke some questions in your mind. Isn't positive generally related with "happy," "upbeat," "fun," or "not negative?" Although this is the popular premise, it is an incorrect interpretation and one that can keep many from further exploring the unlimited potential of students. Many educational researchers have confirmed that a positive environment is the most conducive for maximum learning results. Immediately our minds conjure up these visions of classes filled with frivolity and unrealistic happiness in a contrived situation overflowing with artificial sunshine, which we are certain is reserved for the carefully chosen study group and definitely is impossible in the realm of everyday teaching. Therefore, we dismiss the possibility of what a positive approach could mean to our students, our program, and ourselves, and carelessly conclude that it is impractical, idealistic, and has no application in the real world of education. Yet, when we study outstanding schools across the nation, there is one common theme: everything is based on a positive foundation.

We have all heard the story of the young man who studied for an upcoming math test. After several unsuccessful attempts to master fractions, he threw down his book and announced in disgust, "I'm going to really mess up on this test tomorrow!" Jumping to his feet, his eager father reprimanded, "You must be positive!" And the student retorted, "You're right! I'm positive I'm going to really mess up on this test tomorrow!"

In this case, the young man was really dealing with the essence of what positive is all about. On the other hand, his father was offering a weak (at best) solution to his son's predicament; just "thinking" it is going to get better is self-deception at the highest level.

Our friend Webster defines positive as "constituting a motion which is definite, unyielding, certain in its pattern; not fictitious, real, logically affirmative."

Doesn't this also describe the attributes of a master teacher? Think about your most effective and influential mentors; didn't they bring these same positive traits to the learning process? Now let's go one step further and analyze our own teaching efforts.

Do we constintute a definate forward motion? Let's not confuse filling up time with information as definite forward motion. Although spontaneity is always a signature of a fine teacher, it must be above and beyond the careful planning of each day's goals.

Are we unyielding and certain in our patterns? When we settle for less than excellence, that's exactly what we get. It is important that our students understand our level of expectation. In truth, they do. Simply follow them from one class to the next, and observe their behavior change according to the expectations of the teacher.

Are we non-fictitious, real and logically affirmative? We have all fallen into the trap of being unrealistic. (Though we have fulfilled the non-yielding aspect of our positive definition, we have violated the "real" issue.) And when we address the area of the logically affirmative, we find this is the pivotal point of judgment that separates the good teachers from the positively great ones.

It is pointless (and maybe even detrimental) to affirm anyone who has not accomplished the given task or assignment. That certainly doesn't mean we stop encouraging, inspiring, or supporting them, but we must be honest. Learn the fine art of correcting a person's efforts without damaging his or her self-image. To keep from hurting a student's feelings, we are often tempted to lower the standards so they will feel the accomplishment of the goal, and, as a result, raise their self-esteem. (It also means we do not have to confront the situation and the aftermath of emotion that comes with personal disappointment, so the path of least resistance seems to be an inviting option.)

Unfortunately, the short-lived pseudo-satisfaction is quickly replaced by the understanding that we shifted the rules in the middle of the game. Lowering expectations often backfires and leaves the student with a sense of false security about the integrity of the original goals. (Remember when you were very young and played checkers with an adult who let you win? There was an empty feeling of self-doubt, wasn't there?) Conversely, when we fall short but are met with the "affirmative logic" to immediately go back to the drawing board, hone our techniques and skills, and reach deeper into our creative potential, then the disappointment of not achieving the desired goal is replaced with the drive to try it again, knowing there will be a higher level of self-improvement that will honestly and positively raise one's self-esteem. Now that is positive teaching.

When we begin each new school year, we have new students, a new mix of personalities, and an opportunity to put some fresh new thoughts and ideas into practice. There is no second chance at a first impression. What better time to get serious about being positive?!

Chapter 16

Action: The Key to Motivation

Ability is rated by what is finished, not what is started.

"Motivation—where can I buy some?"

"They never seem to reach their full potential. Just one time I wish they would all give 100 percent"

"This year's class has so much talent, but we're having an attitude problem!"

Sound familiar? Ever made any of the above statements to your colleagues? To your spouse? To yourself? It really doesn't make a whole lot of difference if a group is blessed with oceans of talent if they are not motivated to actualize it. Even the best student can be a detriment to the class if his or her attitude is negative, causing a cooperation/communication barrier.

The truth is: we cannot give students motivation. (Most of us have to muster up our finest efforts just to create our own supply!) What we can do is set the example and point out "thinking habits" that serve as a basis for having a positive attitude. As a result, people can choose to be motivated.

"People behave according to how they feel, not what they know." Psychologists have told us this for years, yet many people continue to ignore this reality. When students "feel good" about themselves, they perform accordingly.

(Unfortunately, the inverse of this "law" is also true: low self-esteem produces mediocre-to-poor results.) In our haste to be outstanding educators, we may have overlooked one of the "key" ingredients: creating a "good feeling" in the classroom.

Take a brief moment and remove yourself as "the teacher" of your group. Recreate yourself as a "new student" getting ready to spend your first day in "your" class. Now walk into the room. How does it make you feel? Does the room give a feeling of warmth and care? Do you feel as though you are in an environment that asks for and supports your finest effort? Do you and your fellow students sense that it is a place where you want to invest your time and energy?

Be careful not to confuse "neatness" with a "caring atmosphere." We have all been in rooms that were so organized and clean they felt sterile. At the same time, there is a lot to be said for the security we all feel in "organization." Entering a room that looks like the latest cyclone disaster is not good. In other words, part of a positive attitude can be handled by "setting the stage." The environment must be conducive to promote and exemplify your goals!

What is acceptable behavior in the classroom? We are all creatures of habit. Whatever actions we see around us, we tend to become: language, topics, focus, physical behavior, and yes, even attitude! We all reflect our environment. Therefore, if it is acceptable to throw things around the room, then it is obviously all right to destroy furniture, scar the walls, graffiti the rooms, and use the teacher's room as a public dump. When energy is not focused, the options are limitless! Do we motivate to support "pride" or simply threaten to insure survival?

How is your attitude as you look through your new set of student eyes? Do you feel you are wanted? Do you feel you can really make a difference? What will be the reward for your attention and effort?

How about the actual class? Did you learn anything? Was there an experience that made you feel good about yourself? Was there a feeling of cooperation and commonality with the other students? Did an attitude of "we/us" prevail as opposed to a selfish "I/me" attitude? Did you really "get into it" or were you just "hanging out" until the class was done?

When we allow ourselves the opportunity to mentally experience being in a group, solutions to the various motivational attitude problems become clear. In many cases, the problems really can be defined and, in turn, lead you to the solutions. It is difficult to find a solution when the problem isn't clear!

Only teachers who really want the motivation of the group to be high will go through this sometimes-painful process. It is a matter of self-evaluation that is threatening to anyone who is insecure. Those people who don't want to meet the challenge simply "blame" the circumstances and spend fruitless energy defending the fact that their students "simply aren't motivated."

For most students, it's not a case of being unmotivated. Everyone is motivated. It's more a case of being motivated to put the energies where they will pay off. What is the payoff for extra study? The trouble is that the rewards we can offer are intangible: pride, self-esteem, integrity, expression, family, care, serving, and sharing. Our value system doesn't always recognize these rewards. In this day and age of instant gratification, we must compete with sports cars, fashionable clothes, MTV, and that frightening peer pressure. With that in mind, we quickly see that part of the task at hand is the education of the value of intangible rewards. When we don't "live" with these values in our own lives, we quickly forget them. Our own energy becomes misdirected, and the "I/me" philosophy takes over once again. "If you show me how happy a motivated/positive person is, I just might try it myself!" That could be a great payoff. It would motivate me!

Motivation comes either from fear or desire. More than likely, you are passing your own motivational source onto your students. We all know fear will work and is very effective for immediate results. It is also something that prepares us for traumatic experiences we will face in life. However, students who work under constant fear tend to study "in spite of" instead of "as a result of." Use fear motivation with great caution!

Desire, on the other hand, tends to remove "set limits." Through this, we open up a whole new level of personal creativity and all the benefits that come from being creative: self-expression, feelings of contribution, personal pride, high self-esteem, etc. "Motivation by desire" promotes the exact qualities that we are offering as a payoff for the student's commitment to the class. Two plus two equals four!

Now let's go back to those original statements and see if we can come to some conclusions.

1. You don't need to buy any motivation: you've got all you could possibly want. It's just a matter of getting it focused in the direction that will produce excellence.

2. The art of focus is never complete: it is ongoing. One must be on the lookout at all times to find one more place to gain momentum. The worst thing to do is ignore it. Stay on it!

3. To get 100 percent effort from any group, it is necessary to make people feel good about themselves. To expect several (sometimes hundreds) of students all to have a "joyous day" at the same time so they will do well on a test is like betting against Murphy's Law. Hoping the good feelings will just happen is simply not a good use of hope. Be aware that society is bombarded with negatives, from television to our own educational system. We have learned to survive on what not to do. Therefore, a major part of our teaching should include methods and processes that create good feelings—yes, even for ourselves. We should feel good about our work. When you feel good, you give 100 percent.

We all have great potential, and we all have attitude problems. The most effective cure for a negative attitude is to create some kind of action; not only does it stimulate motion, but it also consumes the time that might be directed toward thinking about "how bad things are."

Potential that is not actualized cannot serve others; it cannot create action. It is like having money in the bank but no way to withdraw it. When any group becomes dormant, it is a certainty that there is some kind of attitude problem. Without action to offset the attitude problem, it will continue and usually get worse.

The formula is simple. Action causes motivation, which can create and actualize potential. Don't react: act!

Observe outstanding organizations, and notice the common factors of success: busy schedules, constant preparation, a desire to refine and make things better, intensity in all facets of the operation, enthusiasm at all levels, a sense of "family" and group purpose, lots of action, lots of communication, even controversy, high levels of productivity, people who care!

Motivation is an exciting and necessary part of any classroom: it is the "oil that runs the machine of progress and growth." Motivation is our greatest natural resource and the supply is endless. More important, this wealth is available to everyone.

The key to bringing this quality to the forefront is within each of us, and it involves a constant search for and belief in our own abilities. Not to accept this responsibility is a major violation of our right to live a happy and productive life. Our students deserve to see us at our best.

It's time to create a little action!

Chapter 17

Criticize in Private, Praise in Public

The most essential factor is persistence, the determination never to allow your energy or enthusiasm to be dampened by the discouragement that must inevitably come.

—James Whitcomb Riley

We all want attention. Psychologists tell us it is the number-one payoff for the human creature. Attention confirms our very existence. In many cases, it tells us we are needed. The need to be needed is one of the distinctions between humans and other animals; in fact, for many it is more important than survival itself. Even those people who say they don't really want attention often say so because it gets them attention. Whether we receive approval or reprimand, we seek the acknowledgment of those around us, and we guide our behavior according to the attention-rewards issued by those in our environment.

During class, a test, or an extra-curricular activity, from the student's perspective, what is the quickest way to gain your attention? By doing something positively or negatively? Which students are extended the most communication? Let's look one step beyond: How does this exchange influence the entire group? Does it motivate the group to move forward, or does it deter the positive flow and hopeful expectations of the all-too-short class period?

For the sake of example, let's say that the quickest way to gain attention in most cases would be to do something wrong. Misbehaving, talking during class, being rude, interfering with another student's performance, not paying attention, and a host of other choices are almost certain attention-getters. Teachers with every good intention of clearing up the problem may bring the entire group to a standstill while explaining the inappropriateness of the behavior of the guilty party.

Haven't we all walked out of the classroom in a state of frustration, trying to justify our actions (or reactions) to a situation, not only preventing any improvement, but setting the class back three periods? Of course, we then have to deal with the emotional residue that is certain to soil all of those in the class. When all is said and done, our actions are usually based on where we as educators focus our attention.

Logic would suggest that we ignore the students' negative behaviors and acknowledge their positive contributions. However, any accomplished teacher is well aware of the fact that the job is to "correct what is wrong." How is this possible if we ignore what is wrong? The skeptic immediately visualizes one of those shallow classes in which the students are given a false impression of their achievements and contributions by a flood of undeserved compliments. Rest assured, this kind of teaching technique would guarantee the demise of any organization. It would be analogous to watering weeds in a garden. Eventually the weeds would consume the flowers.

The other end of the spectrum is the all-too-familiar environment based on fear. The conditions are as restrictive as the personal resistance to the confining demands. The students are programmed and conditioned to do only what they have been told to do—no more, no less. Research indicates that these students have difficulties progressing without the detailed instruction of the teacher and are hesitant to take any initiative or venture outside the "safety zone" because of the possible repercussions.

Both of these scenarios create a less-than-ideal growth experience for the teacher and the students. We all desire the value of group discipline, yet we encourage our young people to reach beyond their present limits and explore their growth potential and talents. Is there some way to have the best of both worlds? Can we guide the students to take risks and investigate new realms of expression without losing control of the group's ultimate goal? Emphatically, yes!

Behavior modification is nothing more than a stimulus-response process. We repeat any behavior for which we are rewarded. In this case, the reward would be your attention. The students who are given the greatest amount of your attention literally determine the dominant attitude of the group. They are the ones receiving the greatest rewards for their behavior—and others will modify their actions to be in line for their fair share of the bounty. Add this proven truth to the next bit of leadership understanding, and new horizons appear: criticize in private, praise in public.

Criticize in private. If there is a need for an adjustment in the behavior or attitude of a student, meet with the pupil privately. Privacy will afford a candid exchange without the entire class serving as a judgmental audience.

One of the healthy byproducts of this scenario is the respect the students gain for you and the professionalism of your teaching methods. When we can avoid the emotionalism often associated with critical admonishment, everyone benefits. Developing this habit may take some strict personal control, but the advantages are beyond measure.

This approach does not preclude those times when we simply need to have everyone put their books down to have a good old-fashioned heart-to-heart. Such times can be some of the most inspiring and focusing learning adventures in our growth. However, they must be used sparingly, or they will lose their impact and become one of those "here we go again" lectures. (How many times did the young boy cry wolf?)

Praise in public. This could well be the key ingredient. How often do we stop a group and publicly praise a student or a group's fine work? Do we ever simply thank them for being on time and having their homework ready? Have we ever made a "big deal" out of the students who took it upon themselves to form an outside study group? Is there much taken for granted and little attention given to the faithful majority who go the extra mile to be on our bandwagon? Are there many opportunities to reward various students for positive contributions, or are our energies always directed to the negative few? These are difficult questions, but the answers can lead us to optimistic and profitable behavior modification, fostering a new path to better classes, performances, and the improved overall attitude of everyone involved.

As educators, we have the wherewithal to determine which behaviors to appropriately recognize and reward—and this is probably the single most important contribution we make to the child. When we choose to criticize in private and praise in public, we are opting to water the flowers while hoeing the weeds, a guaranteed technique for a superior classroom environment.

Chapter 18

The Secret Ingredient of Master Teachers

We cannot tell what may happen to us in the strange medley of life. But we can decide what happens in us, how we can take it, what we can do with it—and that is what really counts in the end. How to take the raw stuff of life and make it a thing of worth and beauty; that is the test of living.

—Joseph Fort Newton

In the field of education, we are constantly reminded of the value of a qualified mentor. This truth is proven by the fact that many of us have become teachers because of a teacher.

Whether it is the extended amount of time we spend with the teacher, or even the personal relationships developed as a healthy byproduct of extra or extra-curricular activities, we know that this class is more than "just another hour in the school day."

Something very special happens in these classrooms that seems to have more of an impact on students than any other facet of education. Those extraordinary mentors were the ones who were always on fire, wonderfully passionate, predictably excited, and extremely enthusiastic about their life's purpose—teaching their love of the subject area.

Most college curricula do not have a class entitled "Enthusiasm 101." Perhaps they should. Where does one learn this personality trait that is the key to effective education? Does it just happen one day? Do we keep learning and adding more data to our minds and then, all of a sudden, enthusiasm appears, and we become obsessed with sharing the information with others?

In truth, most of us learned to be enthusiastic by being in the presence of an enthusiastic person. We became caught up in the charismatic communication of the teacher, and began to emulate this same ardor when we were given our first teaching responsibilities. It is at that point when we discover the "joy of inspired teaching" and the importance of the mission. That process, in itself, will generate enthusiasm.

There are many competent teachers, but those who are most effective also possess that magical quality—enthusiasm. It's indefinable, predictably unpredictable, wildly contagious, and the fuel for exploring the uncharted territory of human potential. All of this comes from enthusiasm, and these heights are rarely achieved without it.

What is enthusiasm? Webster's New Collegiate Dictionary offers this definition: The belief in special revelations of the Holy Spirit; something inspiring zeal forever. And on that same page, Webster goes further to tell us about the enthusiast: One who is ardently attached to a cause or pursuit. The one who gives completely to whatever engages his or her interest. The derivation of the word (*en* + *theos*) means filled with the spirit in the presence of God.

We quickly see the origin of the word has religious or spiritual implications and, through time, has been transferred to modern language to mean a zealous person, one who is devoted to promoting "the spirit" of whatever the chosen causes. This is a perfect description of those select mentors who brought us to the forefront and piqued our curiosity by demonstrating the art of "giving themselves completely to the subject matter."

Unfortunately, enthusiasm is often misinterpreted as cheap theatrics, over-dramatization, or even a substitute for credible information. The vibrant educator who demonstrates this quality may be the target of ridicule. However, the master teacher who can deliver substantive material with a spirit of passion that opens the minds and ignites the imagination is the mentor who makes the difference. It is at this point that the student becomes his or her own teacher, and a peak learning experience is brought to the classroom. Herein lies the "magic moment" when the individual makes choices that will dictate life patterns. All of this happens because of an enthusiastic teacher.

If it is such a positive attribute, why don't more teachers display their fervor?

To be enthusiastic means:
- Standing apart from the masses.
- Putting forth extra personal energy.
- Being willing to deal with the skeptics and cynics.
- Avoiding the temptation to quit or give up.
- Always finding something worthwhile in every situation.
- Living life with a purpose.
- Constantly growing and learning.
- Embracing the bad with as much love and under standing as the good.

That is quite an agenda to complete and one that takes a tremendous level of self-discipline; however, the benefits far exceed any measurable form of wealth. In essence, enthusiasm makes life worth living. The introspective question we must all ask ourselves is: can we afford not to be enthusiastic?

One of our great modern day philosophers and theologians, Norman Vincent Peale, offers these words about enthusiasm:

> Think enthusiastically about everything. If you do, you will put a touch of glory in your life. If you love your work with enthusiasm, you'll shake it to pieces. You'll love it into greatness, you'll upgrade it, you will fill it with prestige and power.

Isn't that what we all want to do with our lives? We as educators have the opportunity to generate enthusiasm countless times each and every day. Bemoaning the fact that we have had 10 percent cut from our budget, or the scheduled concert is in conflict with an athletic event, or the computer store didn't deliver the repaired parts, or whatever, is certainly important to the success of the program, but it is inconsequential compared to the fundamental charge of our profession, our art, our reason to be: to uplift every child we touch to a new level of appreciation and understanding.

Now that is a challenge that deserves to be met with positive enthusiasm.

★ Part Three:
Teaching Leadership Skills

Chapter 19

A Paradigm Shift for Today's Leaders

Blessed are those who can give without remembering
and take without forgetting.
—Elizabeth Bibesco

The entire realm of leadership training has taken a dramatic shift over the past three decades or so. The strong-armed approach to leadership success has given way to the concept of allowing the follower to become an invested contributor to the overall mission. There is a greater emphasis on intrinsic motivation rather than using extrinsic rewards as a means to individual or group achievement.

The cornerstones of this paradigm shift emphasize a win-win concept embracing both the requirements of the project responsibilities and the welfare of the people involved. It diminishes the power struggle often associated with the traditional positioning, turf protection, rank-and-file status, etc. To find success in this modern-day blueprint of leadership style, these four laws of leadership must be understood and integrated into every decision made by the leader; they serve as the foundational blocks of contemporary leadership.

People are more important than titles. The focal point remains on the welfare of the people involved. The leader constantly monitors the overall attitude of the group, ensuring a sense of mutual understanding and synergistic effort based on individual and group commitment to focus on the agreed objectives.

We can't lead others until we lead ourselves. Role modeling plays a vital part in the leader's ongoing communication with the members of the organization. While delegation is still an important aspect of the process, the leader sets the pace by demonstrating the expectations and the standards desired to achieve positive results. The most effective form of leadership is positive role modeling.

Leaders are measured by what they give. Leadership is an opportunity "to give" to those who are part of the group, organization, or ensemble. The position of leadership is a license to help all those who are part of the forum. If there is not a measured contribution to the forward progress of the group, the value of the leader is diminished to the point of being "merely a title carrier."

Leaders assume total responsibility. When something goes awry, the leader immediately assumes the responsibility for the breakdown rather than pointing the finger of blame at anyone else. The welfare of the followers is primary in every facet of the leader's agenda.

Adapting this new leadership consciousness to any classroom experience offers individuals a greater opportunity to "own the group" and accept the responsibilities for the positive growth and development of the organization. Everyone wins.

Chapter 20

A Template for Successful Leaders

Amateurs practice until they get it right;
professionals practice until they can't get it wrong.

As we examine today's most successful leaders, there are some obvious key characteristics that serve as the foundation's cornerstones that we can highlight and adapt to our own situations:

1. **Present an inspiring and compelling mission.** Instead of merely "working to get better," outstanding teachers constantly communicate the group's shared goals. While elevating the standards, they create an ongoing awareness of various ways to support their vision. The long-range goals are always at the forefront of their communication, allowing the students to focus on the self-imposed behaviors required to achieve the organizational mission.

2. **Demonstrate proven disciplines necessary to create group synergy.** The emphasis is on the "power of the people" rather than the strict authoritarian rule of the teacher. The energy of the students serves as the fuel for forward motion. Discipline is an outgrowth of the commitment of the group members; instead of "being told what to do," the students are challenged to develop their own parameters of behavior that will support the program from bottom to top. Positive discipline renewal comes from an ongoing series of group questions such as:

- What is working well for us and why is it working?

- How could we better serve the people, the group, the goals?

- What behavior will best support those around us?

- What behaviors are counterproductive? How can we alter them?

Blame is discouraged; solutions are encouraged.

3. **Put people first.** The young students are the source of unlimited growth and development. It becomes the teacher's responsibility to unleash the knowledge, creativity, and talent inherent in every member. This requires an ongoing interaction among all who are associated with the program; an open and honest line of communication confirms the teacher's concern for the welfare of the students.

4. **Model a high degree of self-responsibility.** The "do as I say, not as I do" theme is not as effective in today's educational setting. It is important for the teacher to take responsibility for mistakes and to share credit for successes. Modeling is still the most potent method of teaching and leading; therefore, it is imperative that the successful teacher demonstrates trust, appreciation, caring, and concern. The master teacher and/or educator understands that it is not necessary to have the answers to all questions, but that strength often comes from saying, "I don't know. Let's find the answer together."

5. **Have high expectations for results.** The modern-day successful teachers are both people-oriented and results-oriented. They focus on the dual task of "taking care of people" and "creating results through those people." While accepting who people are, they do not accept behavior that does not support the goal of quality. This delicate balance is an ongoing learning process; it is constantly changing, shifting, becoming.

6. **Create a culture of quality through leadership/modeling.** One of the most difficult challenges is to establish of a positive learning atmosphere that encourages the members of the group to contribute without fear of embarrassment, reprimand, pain, etc. If the students assume a defensive posture to protect themselves, it becomes impossible to access their creative potential; however, if the teacher consistently models a forward-focused discipline, a remarkable shift in attitudes, energy, and performance can be felt. There will be dramatic improvement recognized in every facet of the classroom environment.

Chapter 21

From Research to Reality

Even if you're on the right track,
you won't get anywhere if you're standing still.
—Will Rogers

Personal development is a way of life for students of human potential. Much like practicing a musical instrument to attain mastery, outstanding educators are always fine-tuning their communication skills and seeking more efficient and effective ways of bringing knowledge to their students. The combining of the contemporary findings of leadership with traditional teaching techniques has offered an exciting new frontier of possibilities.

There is an ever-growing amount of data confirming that the educator can program his or her personality to ensure a higher degree of success in daily classes. Just as a pilot is required to go through a pre-flight checklist prior to flying a plane, the teacher should have a pre-class checklist prior to standing in front of his or her students.

1. Will my present attitude promote a positive learning atmosphere?

2. Are all my thoughts focused on creating an educational experience throughout the class?

3. Do I exemplify the standards of excellence I expect from my students?

4. Am I properly prepared to make the best use of time by highlighting the growth of every student?

5. Have I dismissed my own agenda of personal considerations so that classes will be directed toward serving students in a disciplined format of measured learning?

It is assumed that there will be an affirmative answer to these important pre-class questions, just as the pilot assumes that the airplane is mechanically ready to endure the requirements of flight. However, the mere process of reminding ourselves of the importance of our state of mind and the impact it will have on what can be accomplished during the upcoming rehearsal will afford us the opportunity to avoid any damaging attitude we might inadvertently bring to the rehearsal setting. We demand total concentration from the students and must, therefore, model this vital discipline. Pilots are not allowed to take off without a perfect score on the pre-flight checklist; teachers should have a similar mandate before lifting their students to new heights.

Chapter 22

The Real Key to True Leadership

Our chief want in life is somebody
who shall make us do what we can.
—Ralph Waldo Emerson

How many times have we all heard the helpless statement, "I just can't seem to motivate my students?" That is absolutely the truth! Nobody can motivate another person. We can manipulate, coerce, inspire, urge, threaten, beg, demand, command, plea, order, instruct—but we cannot motivate them. Motivation is, at all times, an individual choice. Knowing this, we can quickly deduct the false data of such a statement as "He is a great motivator" or "She can really motivate her group." Not so! The person in the first example and the person in the second example are totally responsible for their choice of behavior, just like you and me—and everyone else.

If the preceding paragraph is accurate—and it is!—then why are some teachers successful in (what appears to be) motivating students, while others seem to always be lacking in this important talent? If we back up a bit, some fundamental understanding might help make this very clear. Motivation is a derivative of the Latin word motere, which means "to move, to create action." Obviously, we have carried this into our language with motor, motion, motivation. If we want there to be motivation, there must be action; there must be movement. In fact, under close examination you will probably discover most motivation comes after the action. The feeling of accomplishment, the desire to go on, the commitment to achievement, is usually a result of some action. Without the initial movement, there will be little, if any, motivation. As educators, we can quickly describe these great teachers we have seen "in action," and find they almost serve as a catalyst in causing others to "take action." The motivation (movement) is now in full swing. (It's analogous to priming the pump!)

The only absolute certainty of any motivation in our group is to put the responsibility on the one person we can control—ourselves! That is a huge responsibility we often overlook in our daily teaching techniques. The skeptics can argue all they want, but history clearly shows it is always the leader, or teacher, who is responsible for the level of success of the group; herein lies the real key to successful motivation.

There is much to share with our students about this discovery. When students chide, "You don't motivate us!", you can congratulate them on their insight and explain that their own success in life will not be determined by you and some false form of motivation (manipulation), but they must be directly responsible for their attitude, discipline, and motivation just as you are for yours! Now that's an educational breakthrough that can benefit each and every part of their lives!

Although I have never much enjoyed negative people, an individual's attitude, or mindset, is certainly a personal choice, but when one chooses to be an educator and carries this negative attitude into the classroom, it then serves as "the standard" for the students—and, rest assured, they will learn to adapt it to their own behavior. Once again, the mirror squarely reminds us of our need to create action, be positive, set high standards, and on and on. It is not going to happen until we motivate ourselves!

This reality is beautifully described in this magnificent quote by Haim Ginott:

> I have come to a frightening conclusion that I am the decisive element in the classroom. It's my daily mood that makes the weather. As a teacher, I possess a tremendous power to make a childs life miserable or joyous. I can be a tool of torture or an instrument of inspiration. I can humiliate or humor, hurt or heal. In all situations, it is my response that decides whether a crisis will be escalated or de-escalated and a child humanized or de-humanized.

Great isn't it?! Wisdom is always so simple, so direct, so honest! You might want to share this with some of your colleagues—and you know "just the one" who needs to read it, too!

Plato once said, "We will be braver and better if we engage and inquire than if we indulge in the idle fancy that we already know—or that it is of no use seeking to know what we do not know." As educators, it is our "mission" to seek out new knowledge, strive to grow personally, and set the example for those who will follow in our footsteps. The education process begins with us!

Chapter 23

A Straight-A's Cirriculum for Success

*If you blame others for your failures,
do you credit them with your success?*

Our traditional grading system suggests that getting straight A's is the ultimate goal of the successful student. We have all played the game with fervor—cramming before the final exam, spending late hours with study groups, forcing down that final cup of coffee with the test notes strategically placed beside the cup, and focusing every bit of mental, emotional, and physical energy on the cherished A that will guarantee our success as one of today's best educators. Yet we all know this doesn't always prove true. Those at the top of the class don't always prove to be the front-runners in the profession. There are countless stories concerning the brilliant and talented college music major who found the rehearsal room to be a less-than-desirable environment, and who subsequently chose a career in a totally unrelated area. On the other hand, we well remember the student who completed all the required work, but never seemed to be on the cutting edge—and now they are responsible for a model science program that stands as an example of excellence in your region. How can this be explained?

Perhaps there is another level of getting straight A's we often do not see. Maybe there is more to it than the memorization of material and the ability to test well. Let's assume there are several required courses that aren't in the catalog, but woven into the context of the learning experience. The final grades do not show up on the transcript at the end of the semester, but they are well recorded in the minds and hearts of our colleagues and friends.

How well are we doing in these tuition-free, prerequisite-for-success classes in human relations?

ACCEPTANCE 101. This core class is a must for the educator who will be working with students from different socioeconomic backgrounds or multi-religious affiliations. If members of the group have different opinions or personal tastes, this information is necessary in creating a working, productive community. The fundamental theme of "Acceptance 101" centers on the ability to withhold judgment and see all as having worth simply because they are part of the organization.

APPRECIATION 100-Ph.D. Students at any level can enroll in this class. It can be repeated for credit anytime and is often recommended as a refresher course for the aspiring graduate enrollee. The information is not particularly difficult to absorb, but it seems to be easily forgotten during the crises of everyday life. Highly recommended for anyone suffering from a cynical view of the profession. Much of the coursework requires out-of-class participation.

AFFABILITY 400. Although this is an upper-level offering, anyone is eligible to enroll. Formerly titled Cooperation 400, the emphasis deals with the premise that the ability to get along with others is the single most important commodity of our profession. According to some researchers, 85 percent of all problems are people related, and a greater understanding of this will help clear up many of the daily issues caused by personality conflicts. (A prerequisite class for Profession Success—Honors Class.)

ACKNOWLEDGMENT 201. Giving credit where credit is due serves as the entire syllabus for this course and demonstrates the positive effects of supporting the behavior of those who are contributing and showing dedication to the goal. It is suggested that you do not sign up for this offering until you have completed "Acceptance 101" and "Appreciation 100."

ACCOUNTABILITY 000-LIFETIME. The "ability to be accountable" is the sister course of "Responsibility"—"the ability to respond." Students who complete this class will learn to avoid blame and revenge in their professional and personal lives. They will learn the art of completion. Task completion is the number one builder of positive self-image, and personal success is in direct proportion to task completion.

We might entitle that unwritten page in the catalogue "Secrets to Effective Human Relations." The faculty members are the people whom we are with each day. Our grades are posted in the thoughts, conversations, body language, and general behavior of those around us. If we are not satisfied with the results of our efforts, it should be clear that we need to alter our contribution to the classroom of life.

When evaluating ourselves and others, let's not forget the importance of getting straight A's at every level. The curriculum outlined in this article is one we must study and practice every moment of every day. The agenda of self-improvement must become a habit of life. We all have so much to learn; we will be students forever. A person who does not improve is no better than someone who cannot improve. Let's dedicate ourselves to getting straight A's.

Chapter 24

To Discipline or Not to Discipline?

Oversleeping will never make dreams come true.

Certainly we all want to be successful. Success is one of those elusive terms that means different things to different people. For some, it is a happy family or a satisfying job, maybe a cottage at the lake, a positive working atmosphere, a strong financial base, plus many other ideas. But what does it take to achieve, to realize, this success? We have all heard the various clues, which have been passed down from our teachers and parents: the Golden Rule, a solid work ethic, balanced living, a penny saved is a penny earned, don't burn any bridges, persistence alone is omnipotent, treat every day as though it were your last, the more education—the less frustration, an apple a day, and all that jazz. If it all had to be condensed into one absolute quality, I think (this is a personal opinion!) it would be discipline. None of the above can exist without discipline, and when you review your own list of successful people, don't they all possess a strong sense of discipline?

In our profession of teaching, discipline is a must—the discipline required to learn the subject matter, plan lessons, spend extra time and effort outside of class, and to give up some of the "fun times" available to others. As educators, you have disciplined yourselves to go to college, to study, to take exams, and, now, to complete budget requests, year-long calendars, the discipline of disciplining, and just about everything else that comes into your day. The people who make it to the top seem to have this art of discipline down pat. Their self-discipline is constantly being refined. They have learned (through discipline) to make the most out of each and every moment, and they realize life is about "growing" and that all growing requires discipline.

One of the first things I do in workshops is ask what the participants wish to gain from their efforts. The common answers are: "Develop a better sense of motivation." "Gain a more positive attitude." "Learn to communicate more effectively." "Try to live up to my potential." "Feel good about myself." "Discover ways I can help others." All of these can be accomplished with a strong sense of discipline. There are volumes written about each and every subject mentioned; do these people have the discipline to sit down and read them? Do they discipline their time, their energies, their focus, their choices?

One particularly frustrated student found me after a recent seminar and said, "I agree with everything you said, but I'm not disciplined enough to discipline myself!" Well, that is a puzzling predicament. We all have to come to grips with the fact that it is virtually up to us as teachers. Learning self-discipline is a habit just like any other behavioral habit. You don't just "get it" one day; it is a process of guiding one's efforts day in and day out. Even this takes a special kind of discipline.

When we all look back to our best teachers, leaders, and mentors, weren't they all people who created a great environment of discipline? Didn't they demand that you create a higher sense of discipline to accommodate their requests? Review your most successful times in life; weren't they coupled with high sense of discipline?

Too often, the word discipline is associated with punishment, harshness, abuse, restriction, and the like. This certainly doesn't have to be true. As teachers and leaders, we can approach the whole subject of discipline in a very positive and exciting way, revealing a realm of understanding that offers a host of benefits to the student and is a key to all of the reasons for success mentioned in the first paragraph.

Since it is a learned behavior, it can be taught, nurtured, embellished, focused, and even planted or replanted in any person. In fact, the basis for everything presented in the motivational and leadership workshops is generated from discipline. Once this concept is understood and put into practice, everything from that point on is quite easy. The minute anyone slips, the immediate question is: what is going on with your self-discipline? This, inevitably, will bring the individual back on track. Or, if it doesn't, the individual has to take the responsibility for being undisciplined, which means that person will be exempt from enjoying any of the for-the-disciplined rewards. Strangely enough, there doesn't seem to be any age limit for understanding the value of discipline. In fact, younger students seem to grasp the concept very quickly and immediately begin to collect on the payoffs from their positive efforts, while the older skeptics often are very undisciplined about their discipline and, as a result, have a slower success rate. (Once again, the point is proven in this case!)

Rationalization is the archenemy of discipline and it, too, is a learned habit. Some people are masters of rationalization, which makes them minors in discipline. Which are you? Which do you want your students to be?

P.S.—Avoid the temptation to "rationalize" the information in this article so you don't have to face the task of greater discipline!

Chapter 25

The Best Advice Is: Don't Take Anyone's Advice

Knowledge comes, but wisdom lingers. It may not be difficult to store up in the mind a vast quantity of facts within a comparatively short time, but the ability to form judgments requires the severe discipline of hard work and the tempering heat of experience and maturity. **—Calvin Coolidge**

There is more to the title of this chapter than meets the eye. We all get advice, whether or not we want it. Likewise, we give advice whether or not people want it. Everyone shares information and offers thoughts about what to do and certainly what not to do. A good friend once told me, "Advice is worth about what it costs. Nothing!" (I thought that was good advice.)

Advice never really rings true until a set of circumstances occurs that proves the reality of the advice, e.g., "Don't put your hand in the fire; it will burn." (Oh, sure. Then we put our hand in the fire, and guess what? It burns.) Immediately we are painfully reminded of the advice we should have heeded. However, we are often given bogus advice. "Run, run, the sky is falling." We immediately cover our heads with our burnt hand only to quickly realize we have been fooled and are now the butt of the joke.

For most of us, advice needs to stand the test of time. If it continues to be accurate time and time again, we begin to rely on it, use it in our favor, and even share it with our family and friends. Solid advice will offer benefits that bring better conditions to life and can help us make decisions for our future.

The best advice I ever received came from my grandfather. Grandfathers usually give very good advice, because they have tried it out for several decades. Their counsel comes from years of research and development, and if they don't know by now, who does? Among the many pearls of wisdom Grandpa passed my way, this one ranked right at the top of his "Clues for a Better Life" list: we become like the people we are around.

He was adamant about this and constantly would point out different people's behavior to confirm his theory. He never believed that water seeks its own level, but that we could determine our level of proficiency by choosing our environment and our associates. His many lectures, though gentle in nature, were frequent reminders of how important it was to carefully choose "the best people possible" to be around. That advice served as the key factor in many of my decisions. It was and still is good, solid advice.

There are so many occasions when a conscious choice of what we are going to do can positively impact our future and the welfare of our students, and much of this depends on the people we are around, not to mention the people we bring around.

For example, if you had an unlimited budget, wouldn't you invite the finest experts in your field to work with your students? Of course you would. You would also create an environment that would expose them to high-quality role models.

However, few people have access to that kind of extra revenue, so a more realistic option is to explore the use of audio and video tapes featuring the experts; or when any influential personalities get within driving distance, you put the students in a van or bus and the mountain is taken to Mohammed. We know the harvest of such ventures will be bountiful and positive. It rarely (if ever) fails. Grandfather was right!

We all have had the experience of working with an extraordinary teacher, and when we are in the presence of such a person we reach beyond our known limits and discover we can perform at a higher level. In truth, the newfound talents and abilities were always within us, but the master teacher triggers something that catapults us (the student/learner) to the next level. The mentor not only serves as a role model, but also imparts valuable knowledge that unlocks more of our human potential.

The obvious question is: could we have done it on our own? The answer is yes, but we must then ask, *would* we have done it on our own? According to Grandpa's advice, the due credit must be assigned to the personal teacher we were around.

One of the greatest contributions we can offer our students is to expose them to excellence in every facet of our academic world. Read the finest literature, train their ears to recognize magnificent musical tone, or watch a video explaining basic scientific principles. Search every catalog you can get your hands on and look for the latest video series by the leading authorities, and then make it a homework assignment to view them, study them, and learn from "the best of the best."

Invite credible clinicians to come and spend time with your students so they can witness firsthand the value of personal commitment and self-discipline. Take them to hear good music in a concert hall. (It is not the same as when it is played through the speaker system in the rehearsal room or through a set of headphones. Give them the authentic experience, the real thing!) Take them on a field trip to a science or art museum, go on a nature hike, or visit a lab. And, above all, when your students have the chance to be in an environment where there are a multitude of fantastic teachers who represent today's most respected professionals, do everything within your power to get them involved so they will start to become like the people they are around.

In a world where everyone you meet has a piece of advice, it is always exciting to discover bona fide wisdom that will never let you down. The fire will burn, the sky is not falling, and we do become like the people we are around.

Be around the best!

 Part Four:
Selection and Encouragement
of Student Leaders

Chapter 26

Student Leadership: What They Must Know

When nothing seems to help, I go and look at a stonecutter hammering away at his rock perhaps a hundred times without as much as a crack showing in it. Yet at the hundred and first blow it will split in two, and I know it was not that blow that did it—but all that had gone before.

—Jacob Riis

Student leaders are a necessity if we expect to have high-quality school programs. The day of the teacher "doing it all" is simply a part of history. Although many people are adding extra staff members to their programs, it is still important that students take on many responsibilities. (The education that comes from this is a real bonus to these "leaders" as they take on the various responsibilities of life.)

Often, however, our enthusiasm about getting the extra help—combined with the eager student's desire to have a leadership position—can create a situation that results in confusion and disarray. The teacher is forced to spend time "sorting through" the problems caused by miscommunications, hurt feelings, overstepped boundaries, bruised egos, irate peer groups, false accusations, etc. Is it all worth it? Wouldn't it just be easier to forget all this student leadership stuff and do it yourself?

Although the temptation is often there to give up on this seemingly endless backlash of problems, we might want to take a closer look at our preparation of these young people for their given set of tasks. So often, student leaders are chosen based on, who has seniority, who is most popular, whose mother is booster president, and on and on. All of these "reasons" certainly have validity; however, the purpose of a leader is to lead. If the selected leaders do not have this ability, then the effort is fruitless. In fact, it is unproductive from every aspect and will cause digression instead of progression.

Many of these problems can be avoided if the student leaders have some guidelines. We have all experienced the student leader who simply is not motivated or assertive in handling the responsibilities. Conversely, there are those who are so aggressive that they bulldoze everyone, including us. There are those who are "afraid of hurting their friends' feelings," and those who "have no sense of diplomacy."

There is no right or wrong way to lead. There are no strict rules because every situation demands a different set. But we can help student leaders with some general "dos and don'ts." This way, the leaders will have a head start accomplishing their goals, and you will avoid the frustration of always redoing what was not done well in the first place or repairing the damage done by an immature misinterpretation of position.

First of all, when students choose to take leadership roles, they must understand this means giving up some privileges. They are now expected to deliver on all the assumed rules of their new position: to be on time (or maybe a little early), to be professional (they are now a role model), to have a positive attitude (their attitude is reflected in all of their followers), and to maintain a high standard of excellence (as they go, so goes their group).

In most cases, they will give up some of their popularity. Jealousy runs rampant, and there are always those who think they can do the job better or should have been the one selected, etc. This is part of leadership, and to let them think the position will be all fame and glory is simply a gross misrepresentation of what lies ahead. Leadership is a lot of hard work and the privilege of doing the work is often the only reward there is. To expect more will lead to certain disappointment!

With this in mind, it would seem advantageous to prepare these students mentally for what lies ahead. We must give them the tools to deal with their peers, adults, friends, and even us. When one becomes a student leader, the communication level adjusts. There is a higher level of expectation and a degree of greater confidentiality. If the "expectations" are not met or the "confidentiality" violated, the trust level needed to develop a good leadership style is destroyed.

Here are some guidelines for traits desirable in a high-quality leader. It can serve as a "check-list" for your existing leaders and as a good pre-requisite for developing future leaders.

High-quality leaders have:

1. **High energy levels**—Because leaders are often asked to "go the extra mile," it is important they have a high level of energy to maintain a busy schedule, to perform last-minute duties, and to be the hardest worker of the group. The followers rarely will outwork the leader. The leader sets the pace!

2. **Good listening skills**—This is such an important "secret to success"! Not only is this important when taking instructions, but it is mandatory when working with others. Listeners are few in number, and we all appreciate someone who has time for us. A great rule for leaders: keep you mouth shut and your ears and brain open!

3. **Self confidence**—A role model is three to four times more of a teacher than a teacher. If the leader is to gain the respect of his or her followers, then self-confidence is a must. None of us wants to follow someone who lacks confidence. We want secure, assured leaders paving the way for us.

4. **High levels of integrity**—Leaders understand the ultimate importance of truth. They will always use complete honesty as the basis for any and all of their choices. Any deviation of this will, ultimately, damage the group.

5. **Sensitivity for others**—Truly great leaders operate from a position of "we–us" rather than the popular "I–me." They are an integral part of their group. They constantly avoid a posture of "being above" the other people; rather, they put themselves in the follower's position and accommodate their needs. They sense the mood of the group, as well as of the individuals, and this atmosphere is of constant concern.

6. **A willingness to fail**—Yes, they admit to being human. They are quick to admit their mistakes and equally as quick to correct them. They never push the blame on any unsuspecting scapegoat but realize there is more strength in truth than in "looking right" at another's expense.

7. **Senses of humor**—Although there has to be a disciplined focus on the goal, it is often necessary to "lighten-up" and allow the followers a chance to relax, laugh, and then get back in action. Humor and silliness are not the same. Humor supports forward motion while silliness restricts it.

8. **Optimism**—They do not react with undo trauma to problems, but realize that within every problem lies an opportunity for growth and forward progress. They welcome problems as a chance to test their leadership and gain self-improvement.

9. **Cooperative spirits**—They realize that most comparison stems from insecurity. Their goal is not to "be better than someone else," but to "be the best they can," thus allowing their group to be the best it can. Competition turns into cooperation and all "competitive spirit" is used to improve the situation for everyone.

10. **The desire to care and share**—They will never hurt intentionally, even though they understand there will be times when individual wishes will be overlooked in favor of the group's welfare. They understand that part of leadership is "taking some of the heat" for those unpopular decisions, and they accept this responsibility with strength and dignity. Their sense of caring is ultimate and their willingness to share every ounce of talent and ability is top priority in their actions.

Is that all? Of course not, but it is a healthy beginning to outstanding leadership. If these ten attributes were a certainty for all of our student leaders, the rest of the task at hand would be simple. We have created a framework for the best, and leaders worth their salt will want to be the best. Isn't that why they wanted to be leaders in the first place?

Student leaders are an important part of any first class school. Our position as teachers offers us a rare opportunity to create a living lab for these special young people who are willing to go above and beyond the call of duty. Let's get them started on the right foot.

Take the lead in teaching them what it is all about!

Chapter 27

Choosing Solution-Driven Leaders

To be a genuine individualist requires a great deal of strength and courage. It is never easy to chart new territory, to cross new frontiers, or to introduce subtle shadings to an established color.

—Toller Cranston

How many times have we heard the phrase "You are either part of the problem or you are part of the solution"? In choosing our student leaders, it is vitally important to select exemplary role models who are solution-oriented, rather than problem-plagued.

Students who wish to serve in a leadership capacity must first understand that true leadership requires an individual to do more than his or her counterparts; it is about serving others. Student leaders are the doers, they are the people who roll up their sleeves and go to work.

Even after an extensive explanation of the personal and group expectations, I often wonder if the hopeful student leader really understands the level of commitment, dedication, patience, and personal sacrifice required. For those students who wish to take on the challenges of leadership, and for those teachers who are looking for the student who has the right leadership qualifications, review the following.

Focus on the solution, not the problem. A gifted leader will seek an objective/solution and then begin to move in the direction of the given goal, rather than dwelling on the current status and all the reasons the organization cannot reach the objective. This comes about by using a clear and concise blueprint of a solution-driven vs. a problem-driven plan of action.

The solution-driven leader spotlights the strengths of the followers and emphasizes what is already working. Instead of quickly pointing out everything that is wrong, ineffective, inefficient, and preventing forward progress, the leader will first make a point to recognize the various aspects of the project (including the people) that give it credibility and make it worth the follower's investment of time and energy. The benefit package must be obvious, or there will be no ownership of responsibility by the followers and, thus, no group cooperation and only lackluster participation.

The solution-driven leader sets a stage of open communication and personal involvement. Too often we look for those we can blame for the present predicaments; such behavior can garner initial agreement and emotional approval, but it has nothing to do with solving the problem. It is, at best, a momentary "feel good" and rarely serves the group or the leader. This leader will create a safe, open forum of communication with everyone and listen to any and all suggestions in an effort to attain a better outcome; in turn, everyone begins to become more involved in the implementation of a plan that reflects the group's thoughts and ideas.

The solution-driven leader keeps everyone focused on the goal. We often sabotage ourselves by dwelling on the opposite of what we want. Noted philosopher Soren Kierkegaard said, "Our life always expresses the result of our dominant thought." If we spend our time thinking about why something will not work, we are leading ourselves to a predictable failure. A solution-driven leader will continue to communicate the desired goal to the members of the group; what the mind can conceive, the person can achieve. We must picture high-level achievement in our minds at all times and be realistic in the assessment of what it will take to reach the goal. This is one of the fundamental responsibilities of every student leader; focus the energy of the followers on the anticipated results.

The solution-driven leader creates energy and enthusiasm. The best way a leader can create energy and enthusiasm for a group is to model positive energy and sincere enthusiasm. This does not necessarily mean assuming the role of a cheerleader or extending shallow, insincere compliments. It merely means demonstrating a genuine care for the people, the goal, and the welfare of everyone involved. A lethargic, negative leader will drain energy from any group. This leader will amplify the problems facing the organization; on the other hand, an enthusiastic, positive leader will infuse the group with the needed energy to move forward and discover the endless possibilities available as a result of group cooperation. The solution-driven leader understands the secret to all leadership, the one aspect over which he or she has complete control in every situation: the ability to choose one's attitude at every moment of every day.

The solution-driven leader creates an atmosphere conducive to effective and efficient problem solving while giving continuous renewal to everyone involved. Being a leader does not mean "having all the answers." Young leaders often think they are responsible for every solution, answer, and resolution; such logic can result in frustration, confusion, and even delusion. A perceptive and effective leader will encourage an ongoing exchange of helpful ideas from those who are part of the group. Every suggestion will be met with genuine appreciation, and the communication will be used as an opportunity to confirm the value of the person involved. (If we inadvertently or purposefully reject someone's suggestions, we stifle his or her creativity and construct a barrier preventing further communication.) Maintaining an open, honest, safe environment for group problem solving is seen by many as the most important contribution of any solution-driven leader.

Young people are often enamored by the "idea" of leadership and the personal benefits they perceive to be a part of the leadership position. Choose those who can comprehend the "reality" of leadership, those who are willing to go the extra mile on behalf of their peers. Choose those who understand that the key to quality is the collective work ethic of their followers.

Chapter 28

The Personal Values of a Student Leader

It is one of the beautiful compensations of this life that no man can sincerely try to help another without helping himself.
—Charles Dudley Warner

When asked who would like to serve in a leadership role in the classroom or in after-school activities, do the students really comprehend the extended effort and energy required to fulfill the responsibilities and agendas that lie ahead?

All too often an enthusiastic, young want-to-be leader will eagerly assume the coveted title only to be quickly disillusioned following several unsuccessful attempts to garner group support while trying to accomplish the given project. Personal discouragement leads to "giving up," and (unfortunately) all future leadership opportunities are avoided based on past experiences of perceived failure.

Do we properly prepare our students for "what lies ahead" when they choose to become student leaders? Or do we simply (and randomly) pick this or that person to fill the given position? Are your leaders selected via a popularity vote, or are they chosen because of their abilities, skills, talents, and intentions?

Leadership is made up of two philosophical components:

1. Leadership is for giving.

2. Leadership is forgiving.

Many young people see a leadership position as the chance to be in charge, to tell others what to do, to delegate work, and to put them in a posture of authority. Nothing could be further from the truth. The essence of an effective leader lies in the student's ability to serve others, to create success for the people in the organization. It is the opportunity to give, to contribute, to roll up one's sleeves and begin moving in a positive, forward direction. Whether it is straightening the chairs, putting the books away, creating a colorful bulletin board, or working with someone on a problem, the leader is the person who does the task at hand. A leader does "what needs to be done, when it needs to be done, whether he or she wants to do it or not, without anybody asking."

The second aspect of leadership centers on the concept of forgiving. When something goes awry (and it will), many young leaders want to react to the situation by reprimanding the followers for their inability to fulfill their suggestions. However, the true leader will forgive the people involved and proactively refocus his or her energies to correct the problem and quickly get back on course. Psychologically (and intellectually) we know that people do not get better by making them feel worse.

All too often, there is a tendency for young leaders to chastise those who fall short on the given assignment; nothing could be more detrimental to the trusting relationship necessary for future success in any leader/follower relationship. The solution is simple: forgive, correct, and proceed forward.

When selecting students who will be working with their peers in a leadership capacity, look beyond their group popularity, their gifts, and even their academic standing. Observe how they interact with others, and pay special attention to those who always are considerate of their fellow students and willing to serve them by going above and beyond the call of duty. These are the candidates who are most likely to succeed as leaders; they "live" the values required of every contributing leader by giving and forgiving.

Chapter 29

Character Traits of a Student Leader

A leader is best when people barely know he exists,
Not so good when people obey and acclaim him,
Worse when they despise him.
Fail to honor people, they will fail to honor you;
Of a good leader, who talks little:
When his work is done, his aim fulfilled,
They will say, "We did this all ourselves."
—Lao-Tzu

Student leaders are no longer a luxury in our educational world, but a necessity. We count on these extraordinary young people to offer their time and energy in the ongoing growth and development of our programs; without them, much daily work simply would not be completed.

Students are usually eager to assume leadership roles, but are they capable of assuming the responsibilities that accompany the real leadership agenda? Do they truly understand the personal price of leadership? The selection process cannot be taken lightly, for the student leaders will often determine the attitude, the atmosphere, and the level of achievement for the entire organization; they are the pacesetters for every student in the class.

So many factors enter into this important choice. Are the candidates competent? Are they emotionally secure? Will they assume a leadership posture both in and out of the rehearsal environment? Can they handle stress and pressure? Are they willing to make decisions that are not self-serving but focused on their followers? Do they accept criticism and learn from their mistakes? Are they selfless rather than selfish? Ultimately, will they serve as positive role models for each and every student? These are not easy questions to answer, but they are crucially important inquisitions, for it is unfair to everyone to assign leadership responsibilities to an individual who has not developed the level of maturity needed to assume the added responsibilities associated with productive leadership.

Over the years of teaching the skills and techniques of student leadership, I have observed so many students who are confident in their abilities and certain they can "do the job" and do it quite well; however, they have great difficulty turning hopes and visions into reality. The results are devastating to their followers, the program, and the per-ceived self-worth of the leader. In truth, everyone loses. How can we, as teachers, avoid this dilemma?

In our urgency to have our students become more responsible and productive (perhaps these are one in the same), we are constantly looking for those opportunities of growth that will allow them to experience the pathway to success. After all, our fundamental mission as educators is to prepare students for the rigors of adulthood. It is exciting and personally gratifying when we see students rise to the occasion, but the penalty of failure has a high price tag in terms of the emotional damage to a student's self-concept. Unlike many other aspects of education, failure in student leadership means others feel the effects of the shortcoming. If a student leader does not accomplish the given task, it can (and often does) have a negative impact on all the followers, and the consequences can range from outward hostility to exclusion from the group. In extreme cases, the wounded student leaders will make a decision never to be put in a similar situation where they will be subjected to such personal pain.

Metaphorically, we do not pick a tomato from a garden until it is ripe, for it will be of no value to anyone. It is impossible to place the prematurely picked vegetable back on the mother plant. Likewise, a student leader who is not ready (unripe) will be incapable of surviving the pressure and stress of leadership if he or she has not grown to the necessary stage of leadership maturity. There is an art to the selection process, and veteran educators are careful to find the students who are:

- **Selfless.** Watch for the students who are always taking the time to help those around them. You can quickly identify this important trait—consideration of others—by simply observing student behavior before and after rehearsals.

- **Persistent.** Tenacity is an attribute necessary for attaining excellence at any discipline. Many people will begin a new endeavor with a sense of positive enthusiasm, but you are interested in the students who "complete" their assigned responsibilities.

- **Consistent.** Most student leaders are at a time in their lives when they are establishing their personal habits and their life values; they are truly deciding "who they are." Dreams, goals, and desires can shift radically from one day to the next. Pinpoint the students who are predictable and demonstrate emotional stability, those who can "stay the course."

- **Affable.** It is often tempting to favor the student leader who is gifted, and this is certainly an important aspect of his or her qualifications; however, it is vital for the student leader to have a healthy rapport with the other students. Popularity aside, the chosen student leader must be recognized and respected by the majority of the group.

- **Honest.** Slighting the truth is commonplace. The student who avoids the temptation to exaggerate or embellish the truth and is willing to accept the consequences that often accompany honesty is a rare commodity. Everyone will benefit from being in the presence of a person who demonstrates such personal integrity.

- **Faithful and loyal.** "United we stand, divided we fall." This well-worn phrase is still classic advice for every leader. The students who are always tried-and-true loyalists are your best nominees for student leadership positions. At this stage of leadership, commitment to the group is mandatory, and any disagreements or issues should be dealt with behind closed doors and in strict confidentiality.

These six personality traits are only a starting point; however, they will establish a strong foundation for the selection and qualification of any student leader. We, as educators, must be sensitive to the overwhelming effects student leadership can have on the development of the individual. We are in a position to help our students create a sense of self-worth that will serve them throughout their lives. We can guide their efforts and energies to ensure a positive experience for all concerned. As their leaders, we have an immeasurable influence on their leadership for life.

Chapter 30

Seven Myths about Leadership

The things to do are: the things that need doing, that you see need to be done, and no one else seems to see need to be done.

—R. Buckminster Fuller

There are countless myths many young people have about the mysterious world of leadership. Before we can define or even teach what leadership is, we must erase these false notions; otherwise, we are simply pouring water into a glass that is already full. The explanation of Leadership Myths might be enlightening to you as well as to students. In fact, it will afford many of the people who would never consider themselves to be "leaders" to come forward and offer wonderful talents and skills that you would otherwise never know existed. This is truly a positive win-win benefit for all.

The Common Leadership Myths

1. **Leadership is a rare skill.** Although there are very few who choose to be leaders, it is certainly not a rare skill. More appropriately, it is a "rare attainment." Research has proven time and time again that leadership can be taught. Every student has the ability to become a leader in some area.

Let us be quick to add that leadership is not to be confused with politics or popularity. Some of our greatest examples of effective leaders focus on people who started out at the bottom of the heap. If one is willing to "pay the price," the goal is within reach...no exceptions.

2. Leaders are born. Society has glamorized the idea of the "born leader" via TV, movies, and the popular "rags-to-riches" stories that serve as an inspiration for all of us. Leadership is not genetic. Although we look at certain people as having extraordinary communication abilities, these are learned skills, too. Those who carry the label "personality plus" work at this endeavor each and every moment until it becomes a positive lifestyle habit. If you are born, then you can be a leader, and that is about the only thread of truth in myth #2.

3. Leaders are created by dramatic events. We've been watching too many "Rocky" movies, it seems! The red-nosed reindeer is a great story with a wonderful message, but it needs to be put in perspective as we go about our day-to-day leadership responsibilities.

So many people say, "Well, the opportunity for me to be a leader just hasn't appeared yet." It won't! Most leaders get their positions through their persistent dedication to some rather mundane and thankless jobs. They do it with such a sense of excellence they are automatically promoted to take on more prestigious assignments. "Nose to the grindstone and out of the air!" 'Tis the road map to success.

4. Leaders are at the top of the organization. This myth probably keeps many from doing what needs to be done because they do not feel they have the vantage (or advantage) to make a difference. We have come to think that a title or label somehow buys a higher level of understanding and makes decision making easier and more accurate. Undoubtedly, it is a benefit to have a high profile if one is to lead, but certainly not a necessity.

Some of our most influential leaders in history were people who embraced their mission with personal enthusiasm and carved their own way to success. Ultimately, the true measure of a leader is determined by the degree of accomplishment rather than the political posturing.

5. **Leaders control.** Unfortunately, we often envision the leader as someone who maintains strict control over each and every situation, not to mention the authoritarian attitude toward the people they are leading. We often find the leader is very much "at the effect" of some rather obscure circumstances, and certainly things aren't always to their liking, but they persist in their goal-driven efforts. There will be people who violently disagree with them, others who do not obey their directions or delegations, yet the leader continues to move forward, demonstrating an undying commitment to complete the task-at-hand.

So often the word "control" implies oppression, domination, coercion, and manipulation. It is important to remember that we only have control over ourselves. If people are "forced" to follow another out of fear instead of personal choice, it is not leadership, but dictatorship. (And history clearly points out the predictable results of this negative hierarchy.) The one form of control all leaders execute is self-control.

6. **Leaders are charismatic.** Certainly there are some leaders who are charismatic, and if you have "the gift" (the literal

meaning of the word) then by all means you should weave it into your leadership style. However, it is not a requirement.

Recent studies have led many experts to believe the ability to capture an audience (followers)— which we have labeled "charisma"—may be an extension of highly developed communication skills that can be taught when the creative side of the mind is unleashed through a series of mental exercises. In other words, we are going to be able to teach people to be charismatic, which may be no more than teaching people the confidence to express themselves with disciplined, enthusiastic presentation skills.

Even the great speakers have stage fright, insecurity blocks, and that proverbial nervousness. However, they press through the apprehension and take a stand. It's called leading!

7. **Power is bad.** Power is only bad when associated with greed and selfish ambition. This myth has forced many to stand back when they have so much to offer the organization. They have heard so many people accuse others of "letting the power go to their head" that they won't take the risk of being put in that same light.

We can quickly cite many examples of great leaders judiciously administering power for the welfare of the people, e.g., Winston Churchill, Martin Luther King Jr., John F. Kennedy, Gandhi, and our great religious leaders.

And power does not necessarily mean control. Again, society has often associated power with tragedy and human suffering. Though there are many examples of power abuse, there are equal (if not more) situations in which power has created a better world, including electricity, laser energy, medical breakthroughs, and certainly the shift we are experiencing in the quest for world peace. Truly, it is the way we use power.

It is said 10 percent will achieve leadership status in their lives. (A recent Harvard project has narrowed that small percentile to 5 percent.) Is it possible this figure is not larger simply because people are choosing not to be leaders? And, if that is so, are they not making this choice built on some misconceptions, preconceptions, and/or bad information about "what it takes"? Apparently so.

Teaching and explaining the Seven Myths of Leadership might open the door of opportunity to many of you and your students. It is amazing how many have already given up any notion of ever being a leader because of their sincere belief in one of the above fabrications. Here is a chance to unleash a wonderful source of possibilities and involve more "leaders" at a higher level of responsibility.

I am sure if you post this chapter on the bulletin board, you will have several students curiously reading its message to be followed by some thought-provoking conversation. Encourage this! It is healthy beyond measure. And, most important, it will build the self-image of that quiet student who has been avoiding any form of leadership because of a fear of "not having what it takes."

Everyone has a special gift. Sharing that gift with others is the key to enjoying its full value. And since we cannot lead others until we lead ourselves, it is time to make the most of our lives by removing the myths and taking the lead.

About the Author

Tim Lautzenheiser is known in the music education world as a teacher, clinician, author, composer, consultant, adjudicator, and, above all, a trusted friend to anyone interested in working with young people in developing a desire for excellence.

His own career involves ten years of successful college band directing at Northern Michigan University, the University of Missouri, and New Mexico State University. During this time, Tim developed highly acclaimed groups in all areas of the instrumental and vocal field.

Following three years in the music industry, he created Attitude Concepts for Today, an organization designed to manage the many requests for workshops, seminars, and convention speaking engagements on positive attitude and effective leadership training. He presently holds the Earl Dunn Distinguished Lecturer position at Ball State University. Tim is also the director of education for Conn-Selmer, and he serves as the national spokesperson for MENC's "Make a Difference with Music" program.

Tim's other books published by GIA Publications, *The Art of Successful Teaching: A Blend of Content & Context, The Joy of Inspired Teaching*, and *Music Advocacy and Student Leadership: Key Components of Every Successful Music Program* are best sellers in the music profession. He is also coauthor of Hal Leonard's popular band method *Essential Elements* as well as the creator of the highly acclaimed Director's Communication Kits.

Tim is a graduate of Ball State University and the University of Alabama. He was awarded an honorary doctorate from VanderCook College of Music. Additional awards include the distinguished Sudler Order of Merit from the John Philip Sousa Foundation, Mr. Holland's Opus Award, and the Music Industry Award from the Midwest Clinic Board of Directors.